# ISLAM
*is of*
# THE DEVIL

TERRY JONES

Islam Is of the Devil by Terry Jones
Published by Creation House
A Strang Company
600 Rinehart Road
Lake Mary, Florida 32746
www.strangbookgroup.com

This book or parts thereof may not be reproduced in any form, stored in a retrieval system, or transmitted in any form by any means—electronic, mechanical, photocopy, recording, or otherwise—without prior written permission of the publisher, except as provided by United States of America copyright law.

Unless otherwise noted, all Scripture quotations are from the Holy Bible, New International Version. Copyright © 1973, 1978, 1984, International Bible Society. Used by permission.

Scripture quotations marked NKJV are from the New King James Version of the Bible. Copyright © 1979, 1980, 1982 by Thomas Nelson, Inc., publishers. Used by permission.

Scripture quotations marked KJV are from the King James Version of the Bible.

Scripture quotations marked NASB are from the New American Standard Bible. Copyright © 1960, 1962, 1963, 1968, 1971, 1972, 1973, 1975, 1977 by the Lockman Foundation. Used by permission. (www.Lockman.org)

Scripture quotations marked AMP are from the Amplified Bible. Old Testament copyright © 1965, 1987 by the Zondervan Corporation. The Amplified New Testament copyright © 1954, 1958, 1987 by the Lockman Foundation. Used by permission.

Scripture quotations marked THE MESSAGE are from *The Message: The Bible in Contemporary English*, copyright © 1993, 1994, 1995, 1996, 2000, 2001, 2002. Used by permission of NavPress Publishing Group.

Copyright © 2010 by Terry Jones
All rights reserved

Library of Congress Control Number: 2010926534
International Standard Book Number: 978-1-61638-172-1

First Edition

10 11 12 13 14 — 9 8 7 6 5 4 3 2 1
Printed in the United States of America

# CONTENTS

Acknowledgments . . . . . . . . . . . . . . . . . . . . . . . . . . . . . . . . . . . . . . . . iv
Foreword . . . . . . . . . . . . . . . . . . . . . . . . . . . . . . . . . . . . . . . . . . . . . . . . v
Introduction . . . . . . . . . . . . . . . . . . . . . . . . . . . . . . . . . . . . . . . . . . . . vii

## Part I:
## The Danger of Islam

1 Taking a Stand for the Truth . . . . . . . . . . . . . . . . . . . . . . . . . 2
2 The Roots of Islam . . . . . . . . . . . . . . . . . . . . . . . . . . . . . . . . . 9
3 The Spiritual Characteristics of Islam . . . . . . . . . . . . . . . . . 26
4 A Masquerade of Peace and Tolerance . . . . . . . . . . . . . . . . . 34
5 The Vision of Islam . . . . . . . . . . . . . . . . . . . . . . . . . . . . . . . . 52
6 The Spirit of the Antichrist . . . . . . . . . . . . . . . . . . . . . . . . . 60
7 What Would Jesus Say About Islam? . . . . . . . . . . . . . . . . . 70

## Part II:
## Who Is the Head of Today's Church?

8 The Church Must Take Action . . . . . . . . . . . . . . . . . . . . . . 80
9 The Apostolic Church . . . . . . . . . . . . . . . . . . . . . . . . . . . . . 87
10 The Overcoming Church . . . . . . . . . . . . . . . . . . . . . . . . . . . 97
11 The Persecuted Church . . . . . . . . . . . . . . . . . . . . . . . . . . . 107
12 Stories Given for Our Learning . . . . . . . . . . . . . . . . . . . . . 118
13 The Church and the Government . . . . . . . . . . . . . . . . . . . 126
14 The Cost of Freedom . . . . . . . . . . . . . . . . . . . . . . . . . . . . . 134
   Appendix A: The Contrast Between
      Jesus Christ and Mohammed . . . . . . . . . . . . . . . . . . . . 150
   Appendix B: Muslim Claims About the Quran . . . . . . . . . 152
   Appendix C: Blatant Errors in the Quran . . . . . . . . . . . . . 155
   Notes . . . . . . . . . . . . . . . . . . . . . . . . . . . . . . . . . . . . . . . . . 161

# ACKNOWLEDGMENTS

I would like to give special thanks to my wife, Sylvia, whose love, support, and loyalty have made this book possible.

I also would like to thank the members of Dove World Outreach Center for their prayers and support, especially Pastor Wayne and Pastor Stephanie Sapp, Fran Ingram and Minister Dave Ingram. And of course without the strength and encouragement of God our Father, this book and our lives would not exist. To God be the glory!

# FOREWORD

There are few people more qualified to write a book on the culture of Islam—showing the influence and effects this religion can have on a people and a nation—than Dr. Terry Jones. This book will inform and expose.

As a young Christian minister, he and his wife were sent to Germany, and over a thirty-year period built a large and stable church. Young Jones's burden was to reach out to the lost and poor in a significant way. Through the Lisa Jones House Program, Terry Jones and his church members were able to touch and influence the Muslim community with a passion not known before in Cologne.

It was through this outreach that Terry Jones was able to see how the Muslim people suffered under the curse of Islam, and his compassion grew, causing him to focus his evangelizing strongly in their direction. At the same time, young Terry felt the urgency of calling attention to the demonic spirit that controlled Islam, and the stronger he preached against the monstrous evil force, the more he came under attack by Satan, and the eventual destruction of the large church and all the wonderful outreaches the Lord had helped him establish in Cologne, Germany.

As is so often the case, it was not the Muslims who came against the work of God, but rather the Christian community; even many in Terry's own church could not see his exposure of the Islamic demon as good, and this led to the demise of this once great work for the kingdom in Cologne.

Dr. Jones carefully informs the reader of the history, nature, culture, and overall diabolical intent of Islam to destroy all who do not subscribe to their rigid and fanatical rules of discipline—including their own members—especially the women who are not considered much more than a possession who can be abused at the will of the man. Anyone who is not a dedicated Muslim is considered an infidel and must be annihilated. Jews and Christians (Americans) are singled out as the most hated, extending into the UK and most of Europe.

In time, Dr. Jones recreated in Gainesville, Florida, much of the program he had seen flourish under the direction of the Holy Spirit in Cologne, Germany.

From his now new homeland vantage point in Florida, he watched the Muslim takeover in Germany and most of Europe, and then to his great dismay, the Muslims were growing faster in the U.S. than the American Christian community. But even worse, the Americans seemed oblivious to the growing danger of this devilish virus of Islamism under the peaceful disguise of a Muslim religion.

Once again, Terry Jones takes up the cause to inform, to warn, and to educate the American community around him of the great dangers of trying to cohabitate in a "peaceful manner" with their Muslim neighbors, when all the time they are growing larger families with the distinct purpose of a political and religious takeover of America.

And once again, Terry faces the greatest opposition from the Christian community—from both the clergy and the parishioner.

Dr. Jones is directing his wake-up call to the church of the living God; it is the church, not the Muslim, who will give account to God for their sleepy, lackadaisical attitude. This call is not only for intense intercessory prayer, but also for getting involved in the "street," in politics, and in every phase of everyday life, with the distinct awareness that this extremely dangerous foe is not going to go away without a fight. Let your Christian love and light shine, and let your patriotic voice be heard. This is a "life and death" battle for America's freedoms—for the free enterprise system and religious liberty.

—*Jack Coe*

# INTRODUCTION

*Jesus said, "If you hold to my teaching, you are really my disciples. Then you will know the truth, and the truth will set you free."*
—John 8:32

The world is facing a great danger, which, if it is not stopped, will sooner or later be a threat to freedom in all nations and specifically to the United States. This danger is the growing religion of Islam. Although Islam proclaims to be the truth, it does not, as Jesus said of the truth in John 8:32, set people free. Instead, it oppresses and kills.

In response to the dangerous religion of Islam, our church, Dove World Outreach Center, did something radical. In the front yard of our church property, we put up a sign that said "Islam is of the devil." It created quite a stir, and it was all over the news. It has shaken up Christians in general, and especially the liberal and humanistic Christians who water down the gospel. And it has shaken up the silent majority. One thing is sure: We, "the church with the sign," have become less silent.

People in town have asked us, "Why did you put up the sign? Why did you do it?" We did it to expose Islam. Although Islam is masquerading as a religion of peace, harmony, unity, and tolerance, it is very much a religion of intolerance, violence, and oppression. It is a religion that does not permit freedom at all. If you lived in an Islamic country and converted to Christianity, you would be at best put into prison. You would probably be killed. I say these things because they are actually true. I lived in Europe thirty years, and I have been to Africa several times. I have seen the oppression and result of Islam in Europe and in Africa.

I live in the United States of America—a great country, a free country, a country that is worth fighting for in order to defend the freedom for which many people have died. I was born in 1951 in Cape Girardeau, Missouri—six years after the Second World War ended. It was totally different from today;

in fact, the first time I even heard of someone being gay was when I was in my twenties. I grew up completely innocent. I was saved at a very young age, and from that moment on I was a new creation, believing in Jesus Christ, the Savior. I chose to spend my life growing in the Word of God, living by it, and obeying God's commandments.

Soon I joined Maranatha Ministries, founded by Bob Weiner in Gainesville, Florida. Sent by this organization, I lead the church Maranatha Center in Murfreesboro, Tennessee, and shortly after that I was sent to Germany by the same organization. Throughout my entire life I have preached the one and the same gospel by which I was saved. I have never changed the way I thought and felt about God and the Bible. During my thirty years in Germany I preached this one gospel in a successful way, and many, many people were saved and healed through the simple message. The work I started Cologne grew into a stable church that reached out to the poor and the lost in a tremendous way.

After the death of my first wife, Lisa, in 1996, we started the organization Lisa Jones House, a work that reaches out mainly to the poor and addicted people. We called this work after my first wife because her entire life she was reaching out to help those people. For example, at that time we even had homeless people living at our house until they were stabilized and could move on with a normal life.

Our compassion for the Muslim people in Cologne grew. We saw how they suffered under the curse of Islam, and we started to focus our evangelism in their direction. At the same time I started preaching against the spirit of Islam in a strong way. It did not take long before the devil attacked and destroyed the large church and work God had built there in Cologne.

The devil did not use the Muslims to come against us. No, that was not necessary. There were enough Christians who could not see the attack of the devil, and as soon as he attacked, they let him use them to destroy what God had built. In his book *The Vision*, Rick Joyner described how demons ride on the back of Christians, and Christians become the enemy of God.[1] Such a demonic stronghold was able to use good Christians I had spent almost thirty years with to destroy a great work of God. Through my years in the ministry I visited many places and churches around the world, but in my time of need only two pastors stood with me. For me it was like a second, spiritual 9/11 experience to feel the force and violence of a dark and demonic stronghold coming against us and trying to destroy our lives.

## Called to Battle for Truth

The message of the danger of Islam is so important that we at Dove World Outreach Center mobilized our members and pastors to wear T-shirts with the words "Jesus is the Way" on the front, and "Islam is of the devil" on the back. Even our children and teenagers and high school students, of their own free will, wore this shirt to their first class of the week. We created these T-shirts because it is the truth and because it teaches the gospel. Galatians 1:9 says that if you teach any gospel other than the gospel of Jesus Christ you will be cursed.

Each time the children wore this shirt, they were suspended from school. We were thrown out of the football stadium because we were wearing it. The reason given for their action against us was the enforcement of a dress code! Yet, teenage girls run around half-naked, doing what is to us as Christians very offensive and sinful. We have come so far that we put a dress code over freedom of speech if we do not want to deal with the truth. People do not want to be confronted with the truth, but that does not make the truth any less true!

Corporal John Travis Popowich was assigned to 2nd Battalion 1st Marine Regiment Weapons Company 0331 Infantry. He was wounded on April 9, 2004, during Operation Iraqi Freedom in the Anbar Province of Fallujah, Iraq. He received the Purple Heart, Combat Action Ribbon (in lieu of second star), Presidential Unit Citation, National Defense Service Medal, Armed Forces Expeditionary Medal, Operation Iraqi Freedom Expeditionary Medal, Global War on Terrorism Service Medal, and Sea Service Deployment Ribbon. Corporal Popowich wrote the following statement in an e-mail to us: "I served in the United States Marine Corp for four years. I have seen firsthand the true nature of the Islamic religion."

Do you understand what the words *true nature* mean? Do you understand what *firsthand* means? It means that he was there. He was not sitting in the university classroom or picketing in the streets. He was not expressing a theory in his head, but he had seen the true nature of the Islamic religion firsthand. He had witnessed the brutality of the Islamic religion. He wrote, "I have watched women beaten, tortured, stoned, and killed for numerous Islamic petty laws that had been broken." That is what he saw.

Corporal Popowich saw the true nature of Islam, not the appearance of peace and tolerance that is presented here in the United States. He saw the true nature that can be seen in every country that is dominated by the Islamic religion. I believe that if we would have the kind of experience he had, we would reach the point where we would take a stand against the danger of Islam. We would set aside fear and stand together against this evil.

By putting up a sign to warn against the danger of Islam, we are encouraging churches to stand up and, in love, speak the truth and only the truth. Only the truth will set us free, and we as Christians must not hide it. The church has lost its radicalness, and it is mocked worldwide. Islam is knocking at the door, trying to steal our freedom! It is not too late to stand against it, but it will be soon if the church does not take her position and respond to the call of God!

Before you decide whether you like what we have done in our bold warning against the danger of Islam, I ask you to read Part I of this book to determine if the sign in the front yard of our church is true. Is Islam of the devil, as I am so strongly proclaiming? As God confirms to your heart that Islam is indeed of the devil, you must choose what you will do about it.

God has provided all that the church needs to become an apostolic, overcoming church in our society. Part II of this book provides very specific biblical instruction on how we as the church can enter into His plan for us to mobilize in the battle for truth and against the evil of Islam. God loves righteousness, the right thing, and that is why we must preach the gospel.

The Bible asks in Proverbs 1:22 (NASB):

> How long, oh naive ones, will you love being simple minded?

How long *will* we love just being simple and not dealing with the facts and the issues? The words, "Oh, God loves you," come from our mouths so easily as we sing, in the words of the song we learned as children, "Yes, Jesus loves me. The Bible tells me so." But how long will we stay at that level as the world grows more violent and Islam becomes more oppressive? We act and behave like little children while scoffers mock the church and Christianity.

Jesus has conquered Satan, and He has also given the church power to put the devil under our feet as we live here on this earth.

> [Jesus] replied, "I saw Satan fall like lightning from heaven. I have given you authority to trample on snakes and scorpions and to overcome all the power of the enemy; nothing will harm you."
> —Luke 10:18–19

The church has never used this power and authority to influence and save the nations and society. It has used it a little bit here and there for personal reasons, and some have used it more than others. However, the church has never used it the way God planned it—to become the ruling and reigning church, the kingdom of God, "on earth as it is in heaven" (Matt. 6:10). May God grant that this will become true for you and your church.

# Part I
# The Danger of Islam

# TAKING a STAND for the TRUTH

CHRISTIANS TODAY NEED TO STAND up for the truth. When we at Dove World Outreach Center put up the sign in the front yard of our church, we did it with the purpose of pointing people to the truth. We put that sign there to give people a chance to see and hear the truth that Jesus Christ is the only way for us to come to God. No one, no matter how good they are or what they believe in, comes to the Father except through Jesus Christ, the Son of God (John 14:6).

People have asked, "What about those who are offended by the signs and those who are angry about them?" Looking back at the past, has not the truth always offended people and made them mad? It has always done this, because it points to a need for change. Are we not to tell the truth, because people get angry about it? Should we pull back because people get offended? We live in America, which is supposed to be the land of the truth. We should not be offended by the truth, but we should embrace it.

We need to become like the New Testament Christians, who stood up for their faith and died for their faith. They were persecuted, because they stood up for the truth, a message that there is only one way to God, and that way is Jesus Christ. They stood up for a message of goodness and mercy, a message of forgiveness and kindness and hope.

As Christians, we know this message is true because we have experienced forgiveness for our sins. We have experienced what it is like to be healed by the power of God. We have seen God supernaturally heal people in our services, in conferences, or even on TV. However, you don't see this in Islam, and you do not hear of supernatural healings. You do not hear of people being raised from the dead, cancer being healed, or tumors blowing away, because the followers of Islam do not serve a supernatural God.

Our nation has fallen from this truth, and it is time that we return to it. Pastors have become afraid to tell the truth. Here in Gainesville, Florida, we contacted the churches in our community and asked them if they would support us. They did not even call us back. As we started doing this, many people were against us. All of a sudden, however, this changed. Christians are waking up and coming out to show support. Ninety percent of the people who contact us through e-mail and by phone are expressing their support.

While you can see the freedom in Christianity—in the praise and worship, the forgiveness of sins, Jesus' teaching to forgive one another—you do not see this in Islam. A verse in the Quran clearly shows what Islam propagates and believes:

> After the sacred month has passed kill all the unbelievers wherever you find them.
> —Surah 9:5

Now does that sound like a religion free from violence, as Islam attempts to present itself? If you search the whole Bible, can you find a verse that even comes close to that instruction? The Bible includes verses that challenge us to live the right kind of life. It has verses that forbid us to do certain things that are not scriptural, proper, or moral. But, it does not have a verse that tells us to find unbelievers and kill them.

The Bible teaches that a judgment day will come when we will give account for what we have done with our lives. Did we try to spread the gospel, the good news of Christianity? Have we repented of our sins on a continuous basis in our ongoing relationship with God? However, Mohammed said that the judgment day will not come before the Muslims fight the Jews:

> Judgment day will not come unless the Muslim fight the Jews, and the Muslim kill the Jews. And then the Jews will hide behind stones and trees. And then the stones and trees will cry out: Oh Muslim servant of Allah, there is a Jew behind me. Come and kill him.
> —Sahih Muslim, Book 041, Number 6985

Nowhere in the Bible does it talk about such a thing. It talks about sin, being judged for sin, and the opportunity to receive forgiveness of sin. It says:

> For God so loved the world that he gave his one and only Son, that whoever believes in him shall not perish but have eternal life.
> —John 3:16

> If we confess our sins, he is faithful and just and will forgive us our sins and purify us from all unrighteousness.
> —1 John 1:9

## We Need to Wake Up

Since our church started the *Braveheart* show on YouTube, we found, to our surprise, that many, many people have awakened to the danger of Islam.

From within and outside the US, we receive many supportive e-mails. These e-mails encourage us not to give in to the accusers but to continue raising awareness of the danger of Islam. Actually, many people have begged us to continue this fight.

Islam is of the devil. No matter how much people try to make excuses and talk the danger away, Islam is still of the devil. It is a religion that is beginning to take over. In fact, the word *Islam* itself means "submission."[1] We see most of Europe, especially England, already changing. Islam is beginning to move into the laws and the legal system and take over. We see this in the Netherlands, where individuals are already being prosecuted for insulting or criticizing Islam. For example, Dutch politician Geert Wilders was prosecuted under the Hate Speech laws of the Netherlands.[2] When a religion or an organization is able to steal our freedom of speech, it should be enough to wake us up. It should alarm us.

Listen up, church! Listen up, America, land of the free and home of the brave! We need to wake up. We need to learn from Europe—not from their social systems or health-care plans or culture but from what has happened there. We need to take that to heart while we can. Right now we have a chance to stop it.

We are allowing things that we should not allow in America. We have let Islamic extremist groups start camps to train terrorists how to bomb buildings and murder innocent people.[3] It is time to stand up and exercise our freedom to warn citizens against this. Our nature is not one of cowardice or pulling back. Our nature is and always has been one of accepting a challenge, and to be told we cannot do something gives us even more determination.

Muslims receive the following teaching in the Quran:

> Let not the believers Take for friends or helpers Unbelievers rather than believers: if any do that, in nothing will there be help from Allah: except by way of precaution, that ye may Guard yourselves from them.
> —Surah 3:28, Yusuf Ali Translation

> Slay the idolaters wherever you find them, and take captives and besiege them and lie in wait for them in every ambush.
> —Surah 9:5, M.H. Shakir Translation

If we do not see the things taking place right now, what do we see? What else do we need to shake us up so that we will act? Do we only see the little world around us, our neighborhood and small-town businesses? Trust me, when Islam comes to your neighborhood in an aggressive manner, it will be too late to act. By then you will have to become a Muslim, or you will face death. We must act now! We as Christians must come back to the truth of the Bible.

When we wear our T-shirts that say, "Jesus is the Way" on the front and "Islam is of the devil" on the back, people ask, "Yeah, does that really help? Does that really bring people to Jesus? Is that really the right way?" These are humanistic and cowardly questions. The right question is, "Is it true?" And the answer is, "Yes, it is true." Christianity is a relationship with God, and it stands for the truth.

## Let Us Stimulate One Another with the Truth

We live in an educated country where everyone has been taught to think. Now, think: Is Islam really a religion we want our country to follow? Do we want our children to live according to it? The Bible does not talk about killing Jews or Muslims or any other group of people. In fact, it says the opposite. Hebrew 10:24 encourages us to consider, to think about what we should do to fulfill our God-given responsibility to do good. If you read the Quran it sounds more like instruction to think about evil than good. This is why we must take Hebrews 10:24 and do something with it! We must consider and think about what we have to do to stimulate the people.

This is exactly why we put the sign about Islam in the front yard of our church property—to stimulate the people, to poke them with a needle. It causes some type of reaction, just as when you hear an exciting message. We receive many, many e-mails from people who agree with us and know of the evil of Islam and Islamic laws. Once in a while, a Muslim individual sends us an e-mail. Recently a Muslim lady wrote and said she did not understand what could be wrong with her religion. It turns out that she was born and raised in New York City, so she had not lived in a country dominated by Islamic laws.

Because we want to stimulate Christians, we go on the path God wants us to go. It is the path of trusting God and the path of love, but it is also the path of doing something for God. We are called to stimulate one another with the truth, with love, and with good deeds. What is a good deed? It is feeding the poor and taking care of the homeless and the orphans and widows. A good deed is, as Jude 23 says, pulling people from the fires of hell.

This is what Christianity is supposed to do! This is what the old-time revival movements preached. It is what John Wesley, Charles Finney, and William Booth did. These were radical Christian people. The Salvation Army, which was founded by Booth, was so radical that its workers dressed up in uniforms. You knew 100 percent the side they stood on, what they fought for, and who they believed in.

It is time for Christians to stand up. It is time for us to quit blending in.

We must return to our roots, the roots of radicalness. Jesus called His disciples to leave everything and follow Him. He told the rich man to sell all he had and follow Him. The message of the first church was radical. God radically called Saul and changed him into the apostle Paul. He radically took people who were nothing and changed them into mighty men and women for Him.

If you want to know the truth about a religion, you must look into its holy book and the writings of its founder. When we do this with Christianity and search the Bible, we find that the New Testament is full of truth, challenges, rebukes, love, forgiveness, and second or third chances. It offers eternal life. It teaches that eternal damnation is a consequence if you do not accept Jesus Christ as Lord, if you are not born again, if you do not repent and turn to Christ.

Another of the signs we put in our yard quotes verses from the Quran, including a verse that says Jesus is not the Son of God—the only way to God—but just a prophet. (See Quran An-Nisa 4:171.) If Jesus is only a prophet, He cannot save us. Another quotation on the sign, a violent and radical verse from the Quran, says, "Kill all disbelievers wherever you find them" (Quran Al-Tawba 9:5.) This verse is quoted by many radicals and terrorists, who use it as an excuse to support and promote their acts of violence.

The Bible gives us many verses of direction, correction, and encouragement. It also gives us verses of warning. In 2 Peter 2:15, the apostle Peter gave a warning that we need to heed today. He warned about those who were forsaking the right way and going astray. They were following the way of Balaam, a teaching that was leading them into sin. This teaching was leading the children of God away from Him instead of leading them to Him through repentance.

What are we teaching today? Are we still teaching righteousness in our churches, taking a stand and teaching the moral life that God has commanded? Or have we forsaken the correct way? The teachings today are lukewarm and people pleasing. They have lost their radicalness. We contacted all the churches in our community and asked them to take a stand for or against the message on our sign, but they did not. They gave us the teaching of Balaam, the teaching of lukewarmness. They made statements like, "We are praying for all churches." While that is a good thing, we asked them to take a stand on the message that there is only one way to God, and that way is Jesus Christ. They could not stand up and agree with this.

## We Overcome the Devil with the Word *No*

The Bible is the truth. Jesus is the only way to salvation, and we Christians know that not only by knowledge but also by experience. The power of our

God and His Holy Spirit, whose presence is here on Earth now, is real. It is given to help us fulfill the call of God to go into the entire world and make disciples, but the laziness of Christians mocks God to His face. As they sit in their armchairs waiting for miracles, prophetic words, and entertainment, they tell Him that the blood of Jesus is not good enough or not strong enough to change the world.

Islam is of the devil, and Jesus conquered the devil when He died on the cross and rose from the dead.

> Since the children have flesh and blood, he too shared in their humanity so that by his death he might destroy him who holds the power of death—that is, the devil—and free those who all their lives were held in slavery by their fear of death.
> —Hebrews 2:14

However, the church, through disobedience and resistance to God's command to build His kingdom, has failed to use His authority for salvation and goodness. Christians have allowed the devil to spread his evil, and he is using Islam. Later in this book we will follow the roots of Islam back to its beginnings and learn that Islam is a perverted form of the Bible and God's plan to bless and save the world.

Although Jesus conquered the devil, he still has power on the Earth because we as Christians do not overcome our flesh. We have become selfish, self-centered, and fat. We do not want to sacrifice or work. It is so easy for the devil to pull us into sin and destruction; he does not need to do much. He throws in a little bit of offense here, a little bit of sexual temptation there, and then adds a little bit of jealousy. He stirs it up and puts some heat to it; then off we go with words, accusations, and sinful deeds that destroy everything God gave us through the sacrifice of His only Son.

> Likewise the tongue is a small part of the body, but it makes great boasts. Consider what a great forest is set on fire by a small spark. The tongue also is a fire, a world of evil among the parts of the body. It corrupts the whole person, sets the whole course of his life on fire, and is itself set on fire by hell. All kinds of animals, birds, reptiles and creatures of the sea are being tamed and have been tamed by man, but no man can tame the tongue. It is a restless evil, full of deadly poison.
> —James 3:5–8

Everything that is not from God is of the devil, and this is why Islam is of the devil. The apostle John wrote:

> He who does what is sinful is of the devil, because the devil has been sinning from the beginning. The reason the Son of God appeared was to destroy the devil's work.
> —1 John 3:8

Islam does not make a secret of its teaching to kill all unbelievers. It does not try to hide its cruel ways of punishment and its hard line of dealing with people in an unforgiving and merciless way. It never hides its aggression toward the United States or Israel. It wants to force its laws on the entire world. Islam is offending us every day, all the time. It will never stop its attack.

The Christian church, which has the call, authority, and power to stop this evil, is hiding behind political correctness and tolerance toward this worst of evil that the world has ever experienced. The Bible is not tolerant of evil. Yet, when we as a church stand up and speak the truth about Islam, Christians who are tolerant of Islam do not treat us as with the same tolerance they have for Islam. All of a sudden, tolerance disappears when it comes to the Bible, to the truth, and to the kingdom of God! That, my friend, is of the devil!

After we put the signs in our front yard, they were immediately destroyed. Some in our nation, the United States of America, have forgotten that we still do have the freedom of speech. Well, we replaced the signs, and we will continue to put them up over and over again. We will keep on doing this because the only way to have freedom—the only way to have anything—is to be willing to fight for it. We must be willing to sacrifice for it, to pay some type of price. The apostle Peter wrote:

> Therefore, since Christ suffered for us in the flesh, arm yourselves also with the same mind, for he who has suffered in the flesh has ceased from sin.
> —1 Peter 4:1, nkjv

Christ suffered in the flesh, and we will suffer as well if we are going to come against the humanism in our society and change the direction of our nation. We must arm ourselves with the same purpose as Christ because he who has suffered in the flesh has ceased from sin. Have we ceased from sin by saying no to the desire to do something we know is not good for us? Have we crucified our flesh and said no to that which we know is not right? This is how we overcome. We don't overcome with the word *yes*; we overcome with the word *no*!

# The ROOTS of ISLAM

BEFORE WE CAN TRULY UNDERSTAND the severe dangers of Islam, it is vital for us to understand the origins of this system of beliefs. Many people in the West are willing and eager to accept Islam as "just another religion," bringing along all the beliefs and assumptions which go along with our Judeo-Christian society. This is the most dangerous thing we could do. Islam is not simply another set of quaint beliefs, Islam is of the devil. To explore this further, we have to understand the history and the roots of their beliefs.

This chapter will detail the nature of various aspects of Islam and its beliefs, including its cultural impositions, its view of Allah, its prophet Mohammed, and its sacred book, the Quran. Additional information showing the contrast between Jesus Christ and Mohammed, Muslim claims about the Quran, and a detailed study of errors in the Quran, is included in three appendices.

## A Foundation for Violence

Islam had its start in the early part of the seventh century, in a city called Mecca, in what is now Saudi Arabia. Its founder, Mohammed, was born into a culturally diverse trading city, the major feature of which was a pagan temple called the Kaaba. Though his life had a modest start, he would go on to instigate the second largest religion in the world. Before he died, he left a thorough yet incomplete set of instructions for life in the teachings of the Quran, along with the problematic declaration that "Ye have indeed in the Messenger of Allah a beautiful pattern (of conduct) for anyone whose hope is in Allah" (Surah 3:21, Yusuf Ali Translation). With this one instruction, followers of Mohammed for centuries to come would be compelled to live as Mohammed lived. We will discuss the troubling implications of that statement later in this chapter.

Mohammed began his supposed prophetic career at age forty. For several years, he remained relatively mild, and his early teachings were tolerant, peaceful, and unthreatening to the pagan community.

In A.D. 622, however, the direction of his new religion took a dramatic turn for the worse. The Meccans became increasingly agitated by Mohammed's constant denunciation of their gods, and the Muslims fled from Mecca to Medina in what is now called the "Hijra."

The Hijra is so important in Islam that it is considered year zero of the Islamic calendar. Upon arriving at Medina, Mohammed delivered a particularly pungent "revelation." First, Mohammed explains that if anything he says now contradicts what he said in Mecca, then the new statement holds true:

> None of Our revelations do We abrogate or cause to be forgotten, but We substitute something better **or similar:** Knowest thou not that Allah Hath power over all things?
> —Surah 2:106, Yusuf Ali Translation

As he continues in this Surah, we find a progressive set of instructions from Allah which will direct the course of history right up to the present day:

> O ye who believe! Retaliation is prescribed for you…He who transgresseth after this will have a painful doom (v. 178).
>
> Fight in the way of Allah against those who fight against you (v. 190).
>
> And slay them wherever ye find them, and drive them out of the places whence they drove you out, for persecution is worse than slaughter (v. 191).
>
> Fight them until persecution is no more, and religion is for Allah (v. 193).
>
> Warfare is ordained for you, though it is hateful unto you; but it may happen that ye hate a thing which is good for you, and it may happen that ye love a thing which is bad for you. Allah knoweth, ye know not (v. 216).
>
> Fight in the way of Allah, and know that Allah is Hearer, Knower (v. 244).

Mohammed closes this Earth-shattering sermon with a prayer:

> Pardon us, absolve us and have mercy on us, Thou, our Protector, and *give us victory over the disbelieving folk* (v. 286, emphasis added).

For the remaining ten years of Mohammed's life, Islam was marked by violence and warfare. Because all Muslims are required by the Quran to follow the example of Mohammed, is it any surprise that this path of violence has continued in Islam until this very day?

## Separation of Mosque and State

Thomas Jefferson wrote in 1802 about a "wall of separation" between church and state:[1] a philosophy that has permeated most of Western political thought since the eighteenth century. For a devout Muslim, however, no such separation can exist. Victor Khalil illuminates this further by saying that "Islam regulates every aspect of life, to the point that culture, religion, and politics in a Muslim country are practically inseparable."[2]

Mohammed's teachings and actions are the basis of Sharia law in Islam, and this law system goes far beyond the question of morality and spiritual beliefs. If Mohammed did it, so should any good Muslim. If Mohammed taught it, then it is the foundation of all truth.

For this very reason, whenever Islam becomes the dominant religion in a country, it alters the culture of that nation and transforms it into the culture of seventh-century Arabia.

## Seventh-Century Cultural Impositions

In his book, *Islamic Invasion*, Robert Morey explains some of the impositions that are placed on Islamic culture because of Mohammed's teachings:

> Arab Islamic Law: First, Muhammad took the political laws which governed seventh-century Arabian tribes and made them into the laws of Allah. In such tribes the sheik, or chief, had absolute authority over those under him. There was no concept of civil or personal rights in seventh-century Arabia. The head of the tribe decided whether you lived or died.
>
> Civil Rights: Because there was no concept of personal freedom or civil rights in the tribal life of seventh-century Arabia, Islamic law does not recognize freedom of speech, freedom of religion, freedom of assembly, or freedom of the press. This is why non-Muslims, such as Christians or Bahais, are routinely denied even the most basic civil rights.
>
> Dietary Laws: What foods were acceptable and not acceptable in seventh-century Arabia are now mandated by Islam for all people. What Muhammad ate and did not eat is made to be a divine law for all people.
>
> Women's Rights: The oppressive nature of Islam is seen most clearly in its denial of basic civil rights to women. The well-known Muslim scholar Ali Dashti states: "In pre-Islamic Arab society, the women did not have the status of independent persons, but were considered to be possessions of the men. All sorts of inhumane treatment of the women were permissible and customary."

Cruel and Unusual Punishment: Incarceration without due process; the use of torture; political assassination; the cutting off of hands, feet, ears, tongues, and heads; and the gouging out of eyes–all of these things are part of Islamic law today because they were part of seventh-century Arabian culture. To Westerners, such things are barbaric and should not have any place in the modern world.[3]

Muslims are faced with a dilemma: the Quran is so explicit on many of these points that no moderate interpretation is readily available. These cultural impositions are at odds with the United States constitution, as well as all other forms of modern democratic government. A Muslim wishing to live in Western society then, must decide between imposing Sharia law onto Westerners in order to fulfill their religious obligation, or rejecting parts of Mohammed's teachings– something that is impossible to justify based on the teachings of Islam.

## Origins of Islam

To a devout Muslim, there can be no question that the Quran is the literal and exact word of Allah, delivered and preserved without a single error. The skeptical mind, however, will quickly find in Islam an interesting—often bizarre—mix of Christianity, Judaism, and pagan religious rituals.

For many years, Mohammed worked as a traveling merchant. He was highly successful in this and had the opportunity to travel far and wide. Mohammed had an unmistakable interest in religions and philosophy, and while little is recorded about this stage of Mohammed's life, it seems unreasonable to assume that he did not have plenty of opportunity to have long talks with Christians, Jews, pagans, philosophers, and all other sorts of people in his travels. Not only this, but Mecca itself was a center for pilgrimage for all of Arabia, and a major resting place for large trading caravans. Mohammed had countless opportunities to learn about surrounding cultures and religious ideas. Unsurprisingly, we find that most beliefs and rituals of Islam can be found almost exclusively in the diversity of thought readily available to Mohammed in seventh-century Arabia.

In Appendix C, we will examine a number of these borrowings, which Mohammed was not quite able to repeat accurately. We find remnants of heretical Christian teachings and apocryphal Jewish stories which are likely to have been carried along as truth by some of the travelers through Mecca. In this section, however, we will just look at some elements of Islam that are clearly taken straight from the surrounding cultures.

## The Kaaba

One of the great centers of Islamic belief is the temple in Mecca called the Kaaba. It is in this direction to which believers are required to kneel for prayer, and it is to this very location where Muslims are required to travel at least once in their lives.

At the time of Mohammed, and for centuries before, the Kaaba was a place of pilgrimage for pagans, and it housed somewhere around 360 gods. Any person passing through was allowed to add their own god to the temple if they wished to worship there.[4]

Ibn Warraq illuminates further about the black stone inside the Kaaba, which is held as sacred by Muslims:

> We have evidence that black stones were worshipped in various parts of the Arab world; for example, Clement of Alexandria, writing ca. 190, mentioned that "the Arabs worship stone," alluding to the black stone of Dusares at Petra. Maximus Tyrius writing in the second century says, "The Arabians pay homage to I know not what god, which they represent by a quadrangular stone"; he alludes to the Kaaba that contains the Black Stone. Its great antiquity is also attested by the fact that ancient Persians claim that Mahabad and his successors left the Black Stone in the Kaaba, along with other relics and images, and that the stone was an emblem of Saturn.[5]

While Muslims do not profess to worship the black stone, nor the Kaaba, their inclusion in the practices of Islam shows Mohammed's clear interest in preserving the culture and traditions of the people of his day. This reaches so far that two of the five "pillars of Islam" are dependent on this center of pagan idol worship.

## Allah

While Mohammed's proclamation that Allah is the one and only God may have been new to the people of Mecca, the concept of Allah was quite familiar. Allah was the name of the great moon god of Mecca, who happened also to have three daughters highly regarded in the temple. At one time, Mohammed is reported to have even appealed to the Qurayshi worship of these three daughters in order to convince them to become Muslims; a tactic which proved quite effective until others of his followers objected and rebuked him for it.[6] Allah was not considered the only God, but he was extremely significant, especially to the Qurayshi tribe of which Mohammed was a part.

In the words of Noldeke, in the *Encyclopedia of Religion and Ethics*:

> It is an extremely important fact that Muhammad did not find it necessary to introduce an altogether novel deity, but contented himself with ridding the heathen Allah of his companions subjecting him to a kind of dogmatic purification....Had he not been accustomed from his youth to the idea of Allah as the Supreme God, in particular of Mecca, it may well be doubted whether he would ever have come forward as the preacher of Monotheism.[7]

## The Meaning of Islam

According to Dr. M. Bravmann in *The Spiritual Background of Early Islam:*

> [Islam was originally] a secular concept, denoting a sublime virtue in the eyes of the primitive Arab; defiance of death, heroism; to die in battle.[8]

Morey details this further by stating:

> The word islam did not originally mean "submission," as many people have supposed. Instead, it referred to that strength which characterized a desert warrior who, even when faced with impossible odds, would fight to the death for his tribe.[9]

## Genies and Superstitions

> And they assert a relationship between Him and the jinn; and certainly the jinn do know that they shall surely be brought up.
> —SURAH 37:158, SHAKIR TRANSLATION

Jinn is the origin of the English word for genie. They were a superstition of Mohammed's day, and the belief in them reached into the sayings of Mohammed and into many passages of the Quran. The *Concise Encyclopedia of Islam* defines jinns as the "inhabitants of the subtle and immaterial"[10], something like a ghost or spirit in modern terms. The encyclopedia goes on to say that:

> During the Prophet's journey to Ta`if, he recited the Koran at night in the desert and a party of the jinn came, listened, and believed. Later their chiefs came to the Prophet and made an allegiance with him on the spot which is today the "Mosque of the Jinn" in Mecca.[11]

We find not only this, but also that Mohammed was very superstitious. Surah 113 of the Quran reads:

> Say: I seek refuge in the Lord of the dawn
> From the evil of what He has created,
> And from the evil of the utterly dark night when it comes,

And from the evil of those who blow on knots
And from the evil of the envious when he envies

Mohammed's prayer here for protection from magic arts is a clear demonstration of belief in the superstitions of the day.

## Further Influences

Many of the stories scattered throughout the Quran are straight from the Bible. From Adam and Eve, to Enoch, Noah, Abraham, Moses, and Jesus, they are all key parts of the Quran. Stories from three heretical Gnostic gospels also found their way into the Quran. With the resources available to Mohammed, he would have had no way to know that these gospels had been thoroughly rejected as mythological by mainstream Christianity.

Alexander the Great even makes an appearance in legendary form in one of the many loosely coupled stories.

## Conclusion

Robert Morey ties all of this together for us:

> The religious ideas and rites found in Islam and the Quran can be traced back to the influences of pre-Islamic culture, custom, and religious life.
>
> Western scholars came to this conclusion when they asked the obvious question, "Why does the Quran *never* explain its ideas or rites? Why does it *never* define the meaning of such words as Allah, Islam, Mecca, jinn, pilgrimage, Kaaba, etc.?"
>
> The only rational conclusion one can come to is that the Quran does not explain such terminology because Muhammad assumed that whoever read the Quran would already be familiar with pre-Islamic culture, custom, and religious life.[12]

The significance of the origins of Islam cannot be overstated. If all we found were canonical stories from the Bible, then Mohammed's assertion that Islam was the natural continuation of Judaism and Christendom could possibly warrant further consideration. With the insertion of so much heretical material and superstition, plus many ideas that were uniquely seventh-century Arabian, it is impossibly difficult to think that the Quran is truly the infallible, direct words of the almighty God.

## The Concept of God in Islam

Yet another key to understanding Islam is the sum of Mohammed's teachings about who God is. These concepts will bring us a long way toward understanding the true nature of Islam. In this section we will compare and contrast the Christian and the Islamic views of who God is.

## Infinitely Just?

In Christianity, we believe that God is completely and infinitely just. This frames our understanding of God, and the reason for which Jesus was crucified and raised again for our sins. Because God is infinitely just, He must punish all sins.

The Bible boldly proclaims that Jesus "bore our sins in his body on the tree" (1 Pet. 2:24) and that "God presented him as a sacrifice of atonement, through faith in his blood. He did this to demonstrate his justice, because in his forbearance he had left the sins committed beforehand unpunished" (Rom. 3:25). God demonstrates His perfect goodness and justice in the fact that all sins must be punished.

In his essay on the Moslem doctrine of God, Samuel Zwemer explains that Mohammed "saw God's power in nature, but never had a glimpse of His holiness and justice. The reason is plain. Mohammed had no true idea of the nature of sin and its consequences. There is perfect unity in this respect between the prophet's book and his life."[13]

With this in mind, it is no surprise that we find in the Quran that "Allah forgives all sins: for He is Oft-Forgiving, Most Merciful" (Surah 39:53) and that "Allah accepts the repentance of those who do evil in ignorance and repent soon afterwards" (Surah 4:17). Yet we also find that "those who reject Faith after they accepted it, and then go on adding to their defiance of Faith,—never will their repentance be accepted" (Surah 3:90, Yusuf Ali Translation).

An infinitely just God must have a solution for the problem of sin, which separates us from God. In Islam we find no such solution. Allah's forgiveness is whimsical at best. While this often sudden forgiveness may sound nice in concept, it defies the fundamental belief in a just God. For those thinking that Allah's version of forgiveness sounds much simpler and therefore must be right, remember the words of C. S. Lewis: "It is no good asking for a simple religion. After all, real things are not simple."[14]

## Infinitely Loving?

"For God so loved the world" (John 3:16) is a passage of the Bible known to Christians and non-Christians alike. God's love for the world is the very reason that God sent His one and only Son. Islam gives us a very different picture of God's love. Samuel Zwemer explains this further:

> The human heart craves a God who loves; a personal God who has close relations with humanity; a living God who can be touched with the feeling of our infirmities and who hears and answers prayer. Such a God the Koran does not reveal. A being who is incapable of loving is also incapable of being loved. And the most remarkable testimony to this lack in the orthodox Moslem conception of Deity is the fact that the passionate devotional poetry of the Sufis is put down as rank heresy. Allah is too rich and too proud and too independent to need or desire the tribute of human love. In consequence Islam is a loveless creed. The Bible teaching that "God is love" is to the learned blasphemy and to the ignorant an enigma. Orthodox Islam is a religion without song.[15]

Furthermore, consider the following passages from the Quran (Shakir Translation):

> Allah does not love those who exceed the limits (Surah 2:190).
>
> Allah does not love any ungrateful sinner (Surah 2:276).
>
> Allah does not love the unbelievers (Surah 3:32).
>
> Allah does not love the unjust (Surah 3:57).
>
> Allah does not love him who is proud, boastful (Surah 4:36).

Again we find that the Allah in Islam is far different from the God of the Bible:

> But God demonstrates his own love for us in this: While we were still sinners, Christ died for us.
>
> —Romans 5:8

## What Limits God?

God is limited only by his own nature. C. S. Lewis explains that God's

> Omnipotence means power to do all that is intrinsically possible, not to do the intrinsically impossible. You may attribute miracles to Him, but not nonsense. This is no limit to His power. If you choose to say, "God can give a creature free will and at the same time withhold free will from

it," you have not succeeded in saying *anything* about God: meaningless combinations of words do not suddenly acquire meaning simply because we prefix to them the two other words 'God can'. It remains true that all *things* are possible with God: the intrinsic impossibilities are not things but nonentities. It is no more possible for God than for the weakest of His creatures to carry out both of two mutually exclusive alternatives; not because His power meets an obstacle, but because nonsense remains nonsense even when we talk about God.[16]

In Christianity, we find that "it is impossible for God to lie" (Heb. 6:18, NKJV) because "Every word of God is flawless" (Prov. 30:5). Otherwise, "What is impossible with men is possible with God" (Luke 18:27).

In Islam, Allah has no such reasonable limits. Because the God of Islam is not limited by even his own nature, he becomes completely untrustworthy. His word changes, he is inconsistent, we have nothing to go by. The thought that "Jesus Christ is the same yesterday and today and forever" (Heb. 13:8) gives us great confidence in a God who can be relied upon. Islam enjoys no such assurance.

## Grace or Works

The Bible teaches that we can be saved only through the grace of God:

> For it is by grace you have been saved, through faith—and this not from yourselves, it is the gift of God—not by works, so that no one can boast.
> —Ephesians 2:8–9

In contrast, Islam teaches a salvation based on works alone. The Quran likens the day of judgment to a day when all deeds will be put onto a scale:

> The weighing on that day is the true (weighing). As for those whose scale is heavy, they are the successful. And as for those whose scale is light: those are they who lose their souls because they used to wrong Our revelations.
> —Surah 7:8–9, Pikthal Translation

Islam has no concept of grace. There exists no sacrifice for sins in Islam, and there is no way to salvation and eternal life other than good works.

Furthermore, in Christianity we can say "In him and through faith in him we may approach God with freedom and confidence" (Eph. 3:12). In Islam, even the prophet Mohammed said that "By Allah, though I am the Apostle of Allah, yet I do not know what Allah will do to me."[17]

## The Same God?

So do Muslims and Christians serve the same God? When the Quran says, "We believe in that which has been revealed to us and revealed to you, and our Allah and your Allah is One" (Surah 29:46, Shakir Translation), this quite simply is not true. If God truly is the same yesterday, today, and forever, then His very nature certainly did not change from the time of Christ to the time of Mohammed.

## The Prophet of Islam

An investigation into the life of Mohammed is the most eye opening of all. We have already begun a brief description of his life in the opening paragraphs of this chapter, but several additional points are of interest, and a few bear repeating.

### Early life

Mohammed was born in A.D. 570. His father Abdullah died before his birth, and his mother died when he was five or six years old. His grandfather then took him in, and shortly thereafter, he died also. Finally, Mohammed was brought up by his uncle, Abu Talib. Around age eleven, he began working for his uncle in the camel-trading business, and even at this early age he had an opportunity to travel, learn business, and meet many new people. Beyond this, there is very little recorded about Mohammed's life until the beginning of his prophetic career at age forty.

### First marriage

At about age twenty-five, Mohammed met his first wife, Khadija. Robert Spencer illuminates many of the details in his book, *The Truth about Muhammad*:

> Without Khadija, Muhammad might never have become a prophet at all. Fifteen years older than Muhammad, she was a woman of significant accomplishment when they met. She hired him as a traveling salesman to go to Syria and trade her goods. She sent with him a slave boy named Maysara. On their way back to Mecca, in the scorching heat, Maysara saw two angels shielding Muhammad. In Mecca, Maysara told Khadija what he had seen. Khadija was also impressed that Muhammad had doubled her wealth on his journey. She proposed marriage, although she was forty and Muhammad just twenty-five.[18]

Muhammad and Khadija remained monogamous until her death fifteen years later. Khadija also became the first Muslim after Mohammed, and was instrumental in the first revelations which Mohammed received.

## The first revelation

At age forty, Mohammed received his first revelation. Islamic tradition tells us that he

> ...used to go in seclusion (the cave of) Hira where he used to worship (Allah Alone) continuously for many (days) nights. He used to take with him the journey food for that (stay) and then come back to (his wife) Khadija to take his food like-wise again for another period to stay, till suddenly the Truth descended upon him while he was in the cave of Hira. The angel came to him in it and asked him to read. The Prophet replied, "I do not know how to read." (The Prophet added), "The angel caught me (forcefully) and pressed me so hard that I could not bear it anymore. He then released me and again asked me to read, and I replied, 'I do not know how to read,' whereupon he caught me again and pressed me a second time till I could not bear it anymore. He then released me and asked me again to read, but again I replied, 'I do not know how to read (or, what shall I read?).' Thereupon he caught me for the third time and pressed me and then released me and said, 'Read: In the Name of your Lord, Who has created (all that exists). Has created man from a clot. Read and Your Lord is Most Generous...up to...that which he knew not'" (96:15).
>
> Then Allah's Apostle returned with the Inspiration, his neck muscles twitching with terror till he entered upon Khadija and said, "Cover me! Cover me!" They covered him till his fear was over and then he said, "O Khadija, what is wrong with me?"[19]

At first Mohammed thought he was demon possessed and went so far as to plan on committing suicide. Eventually though, Khadija convinced him that it was from God and that he had been chosen to be a prophet.

## Mecca

Because the Quran is not ordered chronologically, it is not immediately obvious which teachings came at what time during the life of Mohammed. Understanding the significance of the timeline, however, brings us a long way to understanding Mohammed.

The first Surah Mohammed delivered was 96. To follow chronologically requires jumping all over the Quran, but the important point is that there were eighty-six "Meccan Surahs," all delivered in the thirteen years following Surah

96. A careful reading of these will reveal much that we would expect to find in a religion that now so boldly proclaims itself to be "the religion of peace."

In Mecca, Mohammed taught that there is only one God; he taught about the coming judgment, as well as heaven and hell; he taught his followers to do good and give to the poor. In this period, Mohammed saw himself as nothing but "a warner" sent by Allah (Surah 13:7)

**Flight to Medina**

As Mohammed continued to preach monotheism and denounce the pagan gods of the Kaaba, the Meccans became increasingly agitated. The very reason so many people traveled to Mecca was to visit this temple and worship the pagan gods housed there. Mohammed's preaching was a threat to their economy. Amidst persecution and threats from the locals, Mohammed and his small band of followers—about seventy at this time—fled to the nearby city of Medina. Samuel Zwemer explains:

> The flight to Medina changed not only the scene, but the actor and drama. He who at Mecca was the preacher and warner, now becomes the legislator and warrior. This is evident from the Koran chapters revealed after the Hegira [or Hijra]. The first year Mohammed built the great mosque and houses for his wives and his followers. The next year he began hostilities against the Koreish of Mecca, and the first pitched battle was fought at Bedr, where his force of three hundred and five followers routed the enemy, three times as strong.[20]

For Mohammed and his followers, the days of peace and tolerance had just reached a sudden end. After the revelation of abrogation, followed by the decree from Allah to fight, Mohammed led his followers into war.

**The last ten years**

If Mohammed had died before leaving Mecca, it is doubtful that the religion of Islam would have existed for more than another decade or two. Ali Dashti explains these last ten years in his book about Mohammed, *Twenty-Three Years*:

> During his last ten years, which he spent at Madina, he was not the same man as the Mohammad who for thirteen years had been preaching humane compassion at Mecca. The Prophet bidden by God "to warn your tribe, your nearest kin" (sura 26, verse 214) reappeared in the garb of the Prophet intent on subduing his own tribe and on humbling the kinsmen who for thirteen years had mocked him. Shedding the gown of the warner to "the mother town (i.e. Mecca) and the people around it"

(sura 42, verse 5), he donned the armor of the warrior who was to bring all Arabia from the Yaman to Syria under his flag.

The beauty and melody of the Meccan suras, so reminiscent of the preachings of Isaiah and Jeremiah and evocative of the fervor of a visionary soul, seldom reappear in the Madinan suras, where the poetic and musical tone tends to be silenced and replaced by the peremptory note of rules and regulations.[21]

Dashti goes on to contrast many verses from Meccan Surahs with those of Medinan Surahs, noting in particular some of the more infamous verses from Surah 9, generally considered to be one of Mohammed's very last:

Fight those who do not believe in God and the last day (v. 29).

It is not for the Prophet and the believers to pray for forgiveness of the polytheists (v. 114).

O Prophet, struggle against the unbelievers and the hypocrites, and be harsh with them! Their refuge is hell. What a wretched destination (v. 74)!

O believers, fight the unbelievers who are near (kin) to you, and let them find harshness in you (v. 124).

Ultimately, Islam was not spread by the careful use of the pen and persuasion with words. This technique yielded no more than a few hundred followers in Mecca, only seventy of which traveled with him to Medina. In the words of Alvin Schmidt in *The Great Divide*, Islam was not spread using the sword of the spirit, but with the "scimitar of steel."[22]

**Wives and morality**

Morality is generally considered one of the major aspects of religion. When we consider the teachings of Jesus in the Bible; when we read the Sermon on the Mount, we find a moral standard that is unparalleled in the lives of anyone else in all of history. So what of Mohammed? Again Samuel Zwemer explains that

Mohammed was not only guilty of breaking the old Arab laws, and coming infinitely short of the law of Christ; he never even kept the laws of which he claimed to be the divinely appointed medium and custodian. When Khadijah died he found his own law, lax as it was, insufficient to restrain his lusts. His followers were to be content with four lawful wives; according to tradition, he took to himself eleven lawful wives and two concubines. It is impossible to form a just estimate of the character of Mohammed, unless we know somewhat of his relations with women. This subject, however, is, of necessity, shrouded from decent eyes, because of the brutality and coarseness of its character. A recent writer in a leading missionary magazine, touching on this subject, says: "We must pass the matter over, simply noting that there are depths of filth in the prophet's character which may assort well enough with the depraved sensuality of the bulk of his followers…but which are simply loathsome in the eyes of all over whom Christianity, in any measure or degree, has influence." We have no inclination to lift the veil that, in most English biographies, covers the family-life of the prophet of Arabia. But it is only fair to remark that these love-adventures, and the disgusting details of his married life, form a large part of the "lives of the prophet of God," which are the fireside literature of educated Moslems in all lands where Mohammed is the ideal of character and the standard of morality. The list of Mohammed's wives will be a sufficient index to the subject for any student of Arabic literature.[23]

The list of Mohammed's wives is detailed further in the book, *Unveiling Islam*:

Muhammad married at least nine women after the death of his first wife, Khadija. Muhammad divided these wives into classifications of "intimate" (*Muqarribat*) and "remote" (*Ghair Muqarribat*). At the head of the list of intimates was Aishah, then Hafsah, Um Salma, and Zaynab. Among his remote wives he counted Um Habeeba, Maimoona, and Sawda. Then come Juweiriyeh and Sufia.[24]

Aishah was reported to be the favorite wife of Mohammed. She was six when they were married, and he consummated the marriage when she was nine.[25] Muhammad was about fifty-three years old at this time.

## Convenient revelations

Mohammed enjoyed a number of exemptions from the laws that he imposed on his followers. Not the least of these is the fact that they were instructed to marry no more than four wives, yet Mohammed himself received a special exemption from Allah in Surah 33, verse 50, to marry as many women as he pleased. The Quran makes it quite clear that this exemption was for Mohammed alone.

Consider also this verse of the Quran:

And when you said to him to whom Allah had shown favor and to whom you had shown a favor: Keep your wife to yourself and be careful of (your duty to) Allah; and you concealed in your soul what Allah would bring to light, and you feared men, and Allah had a greater right that you should fear Him. But when Zaid had accomplished his want of her, We gave her

to you as a wife, so that there should be no difficulty for the believers in respect of the wives of their adopted sons, when they have accomplished their want of them; and Allah's command shall be performed.
—Surah 33:37, Shakir Translation

The history leading up to this verse is that Mohammed had become infatuated with Zaynab, the wife of his adopted son Zayd. At first, Mohammed told Zayd to "keep your wife to yourself," but soon afterwards Mohammed received this revelation and took Zaynab as his wife.

The Quran, according to itself, is supposed to be the exact word of God, the original of which has sat on a table in heaven from all eternity. To many people studying the Quran, it has seemed odd that the Quran would contain so many specific revelations which pertained to, and benefited, Mohammed alone.

**Mohammed's death**

The traditional view is that Mohammed's death was caused by a Jewish woman whose relatives were murdered in one of Mohammed's attacks against the Jews.[26] Because of his rather sudden death, Mohammed had not made any substantial arrangements for what would come afterwards. He had not appointed leadership or set up any specific forms of government for when he was gone. He also failed to gather or put together his various revelations into what is now known as the Quran; this was taken up by his followers in later years. His death was sudden and gave him no time to arrange his own affairs. Without a solid foundation, Islam was soon to break apart into warring factions such as the Sunis and the Shiites. Chaos followed because Mohammed had not clearly spelled out what was to be done after his death.[27]

## Conclusion

Much more could be said about the life of Mohammed. The appendices and the bibliography for this chapter will serve as a reasonable starting point for anyone interested in learning more. It is important to note that this information is not pulled from the wild fantasies of skeptics and modern opponents of Islam, but rather from the trusted sources of early Muslims. We have no need of looking further than this. The Quran and Hadith are more than enough to show that Mohammed ended his life as both a warlord and a pedophile.

In the words of Samuel Zwemer:

> A stream cannot rise higher than its source, and this chapter has already shown one of the sources—the chief source—of Islam. The religion which

Mohammed founded bears everywhere the imprint of his life and character. Mohammed was not only the prophet, but the *prophecy* of Islam.[28]

The fact that Mohammed is considered the ideal man in Islam has caused problems throughout the last 1,400 years. His calls to jihad and his poor moral character have granted license for all kinds of injustice and evil in the name of Allah. While not all Muslims will interpret his life in this way, we must realize that most of the troubling facts of Islam do not lie with Osama bin Laden and other modern-day Islamic extremists; the trouble grows out of Islam's central figure, Mohammed.

# The SPIRITUAL CHARACTERISTICS of ISLAM

Islam, Judaism, and Christianity are connected by the Word of God, the Bible, and they share many of the same stories. You can find many Bible stories in the Quran, presented, of course, in a Muslim context. Without Judaism, Christianity and Islam would not exist. Although Christianity does not hate Israel, Islam does. I liken this evil response to a family in which one sibling is always jealous because a brother or sister is blessed. Israel is God's special child, and He watches over it. God blesses all who bless Israel, and He curses all who try to come against it.

We have looked at the nature of Islam, and we must also recognize its spiritual characteristics. We must understand that we need to oppose it and learn how we can stop it. I want to draw a spiritual picture so that you, if you are a born-again and Spirit-filled Christian, can see the spiritual relations between the kingdom of Islam and the kingdom of the God of the Bible. The kingdom of Islam displays the danger of its jihad, while the kingdom of God is at work through the saving truth of the gospel.

The God of the Bible reveals the reality of His kingdom to those who can hear His voice.

> My sheep hear My voice, and I know them, and they follow Me.
> —John 10:27

It is my personal opinion that Islam appears like the brother of Christianity, a brother who has turned bad. The Bible talks about brothers like this:

- Cain and Abel—the bad brother killed the good one
- Isaac and Ishmael—The promised son was chosen; the son of disobedience and sin was rejected. Isaac's offspring is the nation of Israel, the children of God. Ishmael's offspring is the enemy of Israel, especially the Islamic nations!
- Jacob and Esau—the chosen one and the one who sold his birthright

How is it possible that the religion of Islam not only preaches but successfully enforces a lifestyle like that of seventh-century Arabian culture? In Christianity we have a big problem passing biblical values to the next generation. The church has partially accepted homosexuality, and many youth no longer believe that sex before marriage is bad. Good values and biblical principles are fading away without the churches standing up and calling for repentance. At the same time, the old-fashioned Islamic religion is growing like crazy! The spiritual explanation for this is its unity and purpose.

## Unity and Purpose

The numbers of radical Muslims and Islamic extremists are increasing. However, all Muslims believe the Quran. They have one Quran, and they all follow it. No Muslim speaks against the Quran. This is the kind of unity we saw among those who were building the tower of Babel.

> Now the whole world had one language and a common speech. As men moved eastward, they found a plain in Shinar and settled there. They said to each other, "Come, let's make bricks and bake them thoroughly." They used brick instead of stone, and tar for mortar. Then they said, "Come, let us build ourselves a city, with a tower that reaches to the heavens, so that we may make a name for ourselves and not be scattered over the face of the whole earth." But the LORD came down to see the city and the tower that the men were building. The LORD said, *"If as one people speaking the same language they have begun to do this, then nothing they plan to do will be impossible for them.* Come, let us go down and confuse their language so they will not understand each other." So the LORD scattered them from there over all the earth, and they stopped building the city. That is why it was called Babel—because there the LORD confused the language of the whole world. From there the LORD scattered them over the face of the whole earth.
> 
> —GENESIS 11:1–9, EMPHASIS ADDED

The strong unity among Muslims is very impressive to people in general, and especially to young people. In contrast to the unity of Islam, millions of different theologies and opinions are held by Christians from orthodox, Catholic, and charismatic backgrounds—and many more. People from each background claim to have the right faith and judge everyone else. Our churches have a numbness and religious sleepiness, with all kinds of programs and entertainment. There is a lot of talking, but almost no one really acts according to what he or she says. The message of Jesus the Christ is not real to the people anymore. People think they got saved by praying a prayer one time and that's it. There is no change, no compassion, nothing!

Islam is a fantastic thing for young people who are searching for something real in their lives. Many young Europeans convert daily to Islam, and they enjoy both the action and violence of it. Finally they have a goal that swipes away the boredom of Western civilization, and they pursue it with no idea of the consequences. Islam gives them room to express their emotions of anger and rebellion like no other religion. Muslims evangelize in such a powerful way, and we can learn from them! They are strongly and deeply convinced of what they believe. This is what young people are searching for: something real, even when it is wrong!

Christianity in our Western world has completely lost its compassion. Instead, we have a humanistic surface and politically correct friendliness, which disappears as soon as a challenge, a conflict, or an offense comes along and needs to be dealt with in the biblical way. Sometimes Christians have the hardest time letting go and forgiving. Instead, we tend to judge others and believe and spread gossip faster than you can say, "Amen!" When I look back on my many years of experience in the ministry, it sometimes seems that you find the most dishonest people in the church.

Christians have, surprisingly, lost the fear of the Lord. They live a worldly lifestyle, they lie and accuse, gossip and judge, and they praise God on Sunday morning without any bad conscience or even repentance. What has happened to the radical Christianity of the first church? Those Christians were so convinced of their faith and the reality of the resurrected Jesus in their lives that they created a holy ground on which religious liars could not exist! They practiced the fear of the Lord, because they saw what happened when the Lord revealed His power.

Ananias and Sapphira fell over dead because they lied not only to the apostle Peter but also to God.

> Now a man named Ananias, together with his wife Sapphira, also sold a piece of property. With his wife's full knowledge he kept back part of the money for himself, but brought the rest and put it at the apostles' feet. Then Peter said, "Ananias, how is it that Satan has so filled your heart that you have lied to the Holy Spirit and have kept for yourself some of the money you received for the land? Didn't it belong to you before it was sold? And after it was sold, wasn't the money at your disposal? What made you think of doing such a thing? You have not lied to men but to God." When Ananias heard this, he fell down and died. And great fear seized all who heard what had happened. Then the young men

came forward, wrapped up his body, and carried him out and buried him. About three hours later his wife came in, not knowing what had happened. Peter asked her, "Tell me, is this the price you and Ananias got for the land?" "Yes," she said, "that is the price." Peter said to her, "How could you agree to test the Spirit of the Lord? Look! The feet of the men who buried your husband are at the door, and they will carry you out also." At that moment she fell down at his feet and died. Then the young men came in and, finding her dead, carried her out and buried her beside her husband. Great fear seized the whole church and all who heard about these events.
—Acts 5:1–11

## Rebellion

If you have ever worked with young children in any capacity, you know that you do not need to teach them disobedience. Somehow they know it on their own! If you do not correct them, they will grow wild and rebellious and they will barely be able to manage life when they have grown up. If you try to teach them the right way and train them in the ways of the Lord, they do not follow these teachings easily! Or, take a look at your garden. To grow beautiful plants, you have to work on the garden on a regular basis. Without work, the plants grow wild, and weeds are all over the place.

These examples show that doing wrong comes easily, but doing that which is right requires a lot of effort. Islam gives young people plenty of room to express their rebellion! In fact, following Islam feeds the flesh. True Christianity, however, provides no room for rebellion. Becoming a true disciple of Jesus Christ costs the price of discipline.

> Moderation is better than muscle, self-control better than political power.
> —Proverbs 16:32, the message

In Genesis we read how God created Adam, the first man. God placed him in the garden of Eden and gave him precise instructions.

> The Lord God took the man and put him in the Garden of Eden to work it and take care of it. And the Lord God commanded the man, "You are free to eat from any tree in the garden; but you must not eat from the tree of the knowledge of good and evil, for when you eat of it you will surely die."
> —Genesis 2:15–17

God created Adam with a free will and gave him the opportunity to say no. And as we all know, Adam did not follow God's instructions on how to live and what to eat. He listened to his wife instead of correcting her, and it cost them their spiritual life. They had to leave the Garden of Eden, the place where the presence of God had surrounded them at all times.

This tragic story from the beginning of human history shows how very difficult it is for us to let someone tell us what to do! We tend to feel resistance rise within us as soon as our boss, our leader, or anyone tells us what to do. And even the fact that Jesus died on the cross and made a way back into God's presence does not help much with this phenomenon.

Where does this resistance come from? It is the nature of Satan, the snake, the devil. He was an angel, created by God and given the highest position—besides God, of course. However, he was not satisfied with what God gave him, and he started a war in heaven. He was able to turn a third of the heavenly host away from God, and he convinced them to fight against God and His angels.

> And there was war in heaven. Michael and his angels fought against the dragon, and the dragon and his angels fought back. But he was not strong enough, and they lost their place in heaven. The great dragon was hurled down—that ancient serpent called the devil, or Satan, who leads the whole world astray. He was hurled to the earth, and his angels with him. Then I heard a loud voice in heaven say: "Now have come the salvation and the power and the kingdom of our God, and the authority of his Christ. For the accuser of our brothers, who accuses them before our God day and night, has been hurled down. They overcame him by the blood of the Lamb and by the word of their testimony; they did not love their lives so much as to shrink from death. Therefore rejoice, you heavens and you who dwell in them! But woe to the earth and the sea, because the devil has gone down to you! He is filled with fury, because he knows that his time is short."
> —Revelation 12:7–12

> And He said to them, I saw Satan falling like a lightning [flash] from heaven. Behold! I have given you authority and power to trample upon serpents and scorpions, and [physical and mental strength and ability] over all the power that the enemy [possesses]; and nothing shall in any way harm you. Nevertheless, do not rejoice at this, that the spirits are subject to you, but rejoice that your names are enrolled in heaven.
> —Luke 10:18–20

These scriptures teach that there was war in heaven! God gave even the angels free will, and one-third decided against Him. The only solution to restore peace in heaven was to throw the devil down to Earth. And if the devil was able to successfully convince angels to fight God, he is definitely able to keep war going here on Earth. We as Christians have forgotten that there is not only a God who loves but also a devil who hates! The devil's territory is the earth. As long as the church does not take dominion over him, he is in charge here! It does not matter how much we pray and say God is in control! We, the church, have to put him under our feet. There will be no peace on Earth unless the church takes her God-given position.

The church has become fat and lazy. The statement "God is in control" has become an excuse for many to sit and wait until Jesus comes back. Such Christians might not enter the kingdom of God when Jesus comes back. Jesus taught:

> "Not everyone who says to me, 'Lord, Lord,' will enter the kingdom of heaven, but only he who does the will of my Father who is in heaven. Many will say to me on that day, 'Lord, Lord, did we not prophesy in your name, and in your name drive out demons and perform many miracles?' Then I will tell them plainly, 'I never knew you. Away from me, you evildoers!'"
>
> —Matthew 7:21–23

God is love, and He is also righteous and true. He talks very straight and clear when it comes to sin, salvation, and how to live our lives to please him. God is merciful, and He has made a way for us to be saved. Still, the choice is up to us. We choose if we will turn to Him for salvation.

## Perversion

At the beginning of this chapter I stated that the Quran includes many of the same stories that are told in the Bible. It has the same history as the Bible, although it presents it in a Muslim context. Islam proclaims that the Jews and the Christians stole the Bible and perverted it. In response to this, we must look at the fruits of the Quran—the teaching of Sharia and the honor killing of innocent people by men. How do they compare to the fruits of the Bible, which offers everyone the chance to receive mercy and forgiveness and be saved?

Who has perverted the Scriptures? Islam calls its God Allah, and it has one prophet who legally had sex with children. Many Muslim women have never been honored or protected, but rather raped and killed. All these things have happened in the name of Allah.

John the Baptist, the prophet who called for repentance, told the Pharisees and Sadducees:

> John said to the crowds coming out to be baptized by him, "You brood of vipers! Who warned you to flee from the coming wrath? Produce fruit in

> keeping with repentance. And do not begin to say to yourselves, 'We have Abraham as our father.' For I tell you that out of these stones God can raise up children for Abraham. The axe is already at the root of the trees, and every tree that does not produce good fruit will be cut down and thrown into the fire.... I baptize you with water. But one more powerful than I will come, the thongs of whose sandals I am not worthy to untie. He will baptize you with the Holy Spirit and with fire. His winnowing fork is in his hand to clear his threshing floor and to gather the wheat into his barn, but he will burn up the chaff with unquenchable fire."
> —Luke 3:7–9, 16–17

Jesus confronted the Jews of His day because of their profession that they were the children of Abraham and told them that they were actually the children of the devil:

> "If you were Abraham's children," said Jesus, "then you would do the things Abraham did. As it is, you are determined to kill me, a man who has told you the truth that I heard from God. Abraham did not do such things. You are doing the things your own father does." "We are not illegitimate children," they protested. "The only Father we have is God himself." Jesus said to them, "If God were your Father, you would love me, for I came from God and now am here. I have not come on my own; but he sent me. Why is my language not clear to you? Because you are unable to hear what I say. You belong to your father, the devil, and you want to carry out your father's desire. He was a murderer from the beginning, not holding to the truth, for there is no truth in him. When he lies, he speaks his native language, for he is a liar and the father of lies. Yet because I tell the truth, you do not believe me!"
> —John 8:39–45

It does not matter what we call ourselves to justify our deeds! Any and all who do not honor God as Father by loving Jesus, whom He sent, have the same father—the devil. The devil is a liar, and there is only falsehood and evil among his children. The devil himself is still entirely convinced that he can win against God. He believes his own lies, and to him they are not lies anymore.

We find this pattern in Islam, which, for centuries, has made millions of people believe it is the only way of life, when it actually is turning the whole world backwards into brutal chaos! There is no logic in this way of thinking, only demonic anointing.

We have a strong movement in America that teaches the political and human way to stop Islam. It wants to prevent the Western governments from integrating Sharia law into our Western society. That is, of course, right. However, even if this would work, it would not last. Many Muslims are already in the government and in the military.

Islam is a spiritual force and must be conquered by the spiritual authority of the apostolic church! The devil is filled with fury—the fury you find in Islam!

# A MASQUERADE of PEACE and TOLERANCE

As we noted in the Introduction, Islam is masquerading as a religion of peace and tolerance. But how can we be sure that it really is what it appears to be? To help us determine this, we will examine the fruits of Islam in this chapter. In Matthew 7:16 the Bible says that we will recognize false prophets by their fruit.

In contrast to Christianity, which is a religion of mercy, forgiveness, and eternal life, Islam is a religion of punishment and control. If you examine the Quran, you will find basically no verses on mercy, tolerance, or forgiveness. Instead, you will find evidence of just the opposite: war, violence, and a strong demand for Muslims to please Allah by searching for, finding, and destroying unbelievers.

The Bible teaches that the punishment for sin is spiritual death, but we can have life through Jesus by simply repenting and turning to Him. We can receive God's mercy and forgiveness. God sent His Son so we would not have to die for our sin. We could not pay such a huge debt, so Jesus came and paid it for us.

Islamic teaching on punishment, however, presents laws that are cruel and leave no room for mercy or repentance at all. You do not see forgiveness or feel the kindness of a loving God. The Quran does not reflect a merciful, loving God who is waiting to forgive and restore. Rather, we see the establishment of its holy book as the law—Sharia law! This is a legal system based on the teachings of the Quran—the Sunnah and the Hadith of Mohammed, applied to the community as the legal basis for life:

- Adultery in the US: Adultery is not illegal. A person who committed adultery will not be arrested; adultery is not a crime. In the Bible it is considered a crime, but through the forgiveness and mercy of God there is salvation and new life. (See Exod. 20, 14, 17; John 8:4–11.) Through the years and the development in the Western world, adultery has been accepted and is considered in general as a phase of life people just go through.

- Adultery under Sharia law: Stoning in Islam (Sahih Muslim Book 017, Number 4209).
- Stealing in the West: Stealing is illegal, U.S. law.
- Stealing under Sharia law: In the Quran, "As to the thief, Male or female, cut off his or her hands: a punishment by way of example, from Allah, for their crime: and Allah is Exalted in power" (Surah 5:38, Yusuf Ali Translation).
- Freedom of religion in the US: Constitution, U.S. law, First Amendment.
- Freedom of religion under Sharia law: there is no freedom of religion. "Fight those who believe not in Allah nor the Last Day, nor hold that forbidden which hath been forbidden by Allah and His Messenger, nor acknowledge the religion of Truth, (even if they are) of the People of the Book, until they pay the Jizya with willing submission, and feel themselves subdued" (Surah 9:29, Yusuf Ali Translation).
- Converting to another religion in the U.S. is not illegal, U.S. law.
- Converting to another religion under Sharia law: Al-Razi commentary on Quran, Surah 2:217.
- Equality of men and women in the U.S. is protected by U.S. law.
- Equality of men and women under Sharia law: "Men are in charge of women, because Allah hath made the one of them to excel the other, and because they spend of their property (for the support of women). So good women are the obedient, guarding in secret that which Allah hath guarded. As for those from whom ye fear rebellion, admonish them and banish them to beds apart, and scourge them" (Surah 4:34, Pikthal Translation). "O ye who believe! When ye deal with each other, in transactions involving future obligations in a fixed period of time, reduce them to writing. Let a scribe write down faithfully as between the parties: let not the scribe refuse to write: as Allah Has taught him, so let him write. Let him who incurs the liability dictate, but let him fear His Lord Allah, and not diminish aught of what he owes. If the party liable is mentally deficient, or weak, or unable Himself to dictate, Let his

guardian dictate faithfully, and get two witnesses, out of your own men, and if there are not two men, then a man and two women" (Quran 2:282, Yusuf Ali Translation).

## Life Under Sharia Law

The enforcement of Sharia law on daily life in Islamic countries produces shocking actions. Public executions are normal in Islamic states like Saudi Arabia and Iran. People are flogged, killed, stoned, and beheaded for minor infractions. Islamic law calls for cutting of hands to punish thieves. "As to the thief, Male or female, cut off his or her hands: a punishment by way of example, from Allah, for their crime: and Allah is Exalted in power" (Surah 5:38, Yusuf Ali Translation). A judge usually makes those decisions, but can you be sure that each person gets a fair trail? I doubt that. Because the court systems in many of these countries are based on Sharia law as well, it is difficult for individuals to get a fair trial or what would, in the West, be considered just punishment.

Imagine how our Western society would look if we pursued fornication (sex before marriage) and adultery (sex outside of marriage) and punished offenders according to the same rule used in some Muslim nations. What if those found guilty of fornication or adultery were beaten, stoned, hung, or beheaded? How many graveyards would we need? Sexual sin has become normal in our society, but that certainly does not make it right. It is still sin in God's eyes. Jesus' answer to fornication and adultery is forgiveness for all who turn from their sin and rebellion and come to Him.

In Islamic countries, people do not have the freedom of speech guaranteed by the First Amendment of the United States Constitution. Homosexuals cannot go there and demonstrate for same-sex marriage. Islam's answer to homosexuality is execution; in 2006 two gay teenagers in Iran were hung for participating in homosexual activity.[2] Homosexuality is, according to the Bible, very wrong. It is a perverted life style that is an expression of deep rebellion. Yet, Jesus' answer is forgiveness and deliverance from the force that drives one in that direction.

It is very clear that Islam is a religion of punishment, not mercy and forgiveness. In addition, Islam is a religion that is void of human rights. It is not a religion of equality. The Quran 2:282 is often interpreted to indicate that a woman's input is worth half that of a man's. This is what Muslims believe. It is what their religion teaches and practices.

In Islam, women have basically no rights whatsoever. They are considered the personal property of a man and have no say in whom they marry. They are given away by their guardians, by their parents, without their consent, and they do not even have to be present at their wedding. In fact, they can be married to someone considerably older than they are and not even know it until someone drags them away. This can happen to little girls as young as nine years old.

The Quran in 4:34 condones the beating of a man's wife, and abuse in Islamic marriages is common. The Internet has sites at which men give instructions on the proper way to beat your wife. For example, an eleven-year-old girl was given into marriage to her cousin who was over forty years old. She was terribly abused by her husband. When she ran back to her father's house for shelter and protection from the abuser, her father sent her back because it was considered shameful to leave the house without permission.

A woman can be divorced by her husband by him saying three times, "I divorce you."[3] If a woman is widowed, she lives with the family of her husband. It is normal for widows to suffer rape and abuse by male relatives. If an unmarried woman gets pregnant because of rape, or sexual abuse is exposed in any other way, the woman becomes the subject of honor-killing. Let me tell you a true story about a widow, who after her husband's death lived with the family of her husband's brother. This brother raped the widow every day, and the woman had no protection. Because of the Sharia law, she needed four witnesses to confirm her testimony. One day she got pregnant, and the law would require that her fifteen-year-old son kill her. The widow had a secret abortion and almost died from it, because she didn't have enough money to pay for the anesthesia, and the abortion was done without it.[4] How great is the need of a woman to escape this curse and shame of hopelessness being committed every day to the cruel and evil Islamic law that shows no mercy! How can anyone not agree that Islam is of the devil?

Women in countries such as Saudi Arabia are not allowed to possess a driver's license or drive cars. If a woman walks alone on the streets, she takes a high risk of being arrested, and if she converts to another religion, she maybe subject to an honor killing to remove shame from the family.

As we consider these things, I wonder why anyone would convert to Islam. And where are the people who are standing up for the rights of these women? Where are the Christians? Where are all the women who march for their own equality, because we have freedom here in the United States? Why have women's rights developed through the centuries in the entire world except in Islamic nations? It seems that there time has stood still. Those people still do live in the past. How can this be possible?

## What Is Honor Killing?

An honor killing is the murder of a family or clan member by one or more fellow family members, where the murderers believe the victim to have brought dishonor upon the family, clan, or community. This perceived dishonor is normally the result of (a) utilizing dress codes unacceptable to the family (b) wanting out of an arranged marriage or choosing to marry by own choice, (c) engaging in certain sexual acts or (d) engaging in relations with the opposite sex. These killings result from the perception that defense of honor justifies killing a person whose behavior dishonors their clan or family.[5]

Human Rights Watch defines "honor killings" as follows: Honor crimes are acts of violence, usually murder, committed by male family members against female family members, who are held to have brought dishonor upon the family. A woman can be targeted by (individuals within) her family for a variety of reasons, including: refusing to enter into an arranged marriage, being the victim of a sexual assault, seeking a divorce—even from an abusive husband—or (allegedly) committing adultery. The mere perception that a woman has behaved in a way that 'dishonors' her family is sufficient to trigger an attack on her life.[6]

A different form of honor killing is honor suicide. This is a process whereby a person commits suicide to escape the shame of any immoral actions, for example having had extra-marital sexual relations. There are also documented cases in where other person/-s has pressured a victim to kill himself/herself to avoid penalties for murdering him/her in an honor killing; this practice is known as forced suicide. Over 80 Iraqi women in Diyala province committed suicide, to escape the shame of having been raped. They chose to become suicide bombers to escape the shame; startlingly, their rapes were planned in advance by a 51 year old Iraqi woman Samira Jassim, who confessed to Iraqi police that she organized their rapes so she could later persuade each of them that to become a suicide bomber was the only way to escape their shame.[7]

Honor killing occurs not only in Islamic countries, it happens everywhere where Muslims live. It happens even in the United States of America. Here is a list of some cases of honor killing:

### Zahida Parveen

It was a seemingly ordinary night three years ago when Zahida Parveen, then 30, was asleep in a room with her two small children. Her family was poor, but she was happy with her life with Mehmood Iqbal, her husband of four years. All that changed in an instant when she was forced out of bed, viciously attacked and left for dead, her face mutilated beyond recognition. Her attacker: her 35-year-old husband, who did it because he was convinced his wife was having an affair.[8]

## Ghazala Khan, Denmark

Shot and killed in Denmark by her brother after she had married against the will of the family.[9]

## Rojda, Turkey, 2005

As a 13-year-old girl in Turkey, she was raped, then forced to marry her rapist under Islamic law. Her face was mutilated by her husband's family when she refused to prostitute herself after he was imprisoned for raping another child.[10]

## Methal Dayem—a 22-year-old Cleveland State student

Methal Dayem was shot four times on Jan. 8, 1999. Three of the bullets hit her legs and torso. A fourth passed through the back of her neck and out through her voicebox. She died suffocating on her own blood. And Cleveland police had learned that much of Methal Dayem's family, Palestinian immigrants, were upset with Methal Dayem's increasing independence, especially since she backed out of an arranged marriage a year before.[11]

## Rudayena Jemael with Her Son and Killer Salim

A woman's death has raised disturbing questions about "honor killings" in certain Arab villages of Israel. According to the tribal custom, a father, husband, brother or son is duty-bound to kill a female family member who allegedly has brought shame on the family. A cultural conspiracy of silence often hides the brutality. Rudayena Jemael, 37, was shot in the head while she slept in her home. There was no forced entry, no robbery. Police say her 20-year-old son is the prime suspect. They think he killed her because she wanted to remarry, 19 years after her divorce.[12]

## Sazan Bajez—Abdullah—Germany

In the Munich court room the mood was dead silence, as a 35-year-old Iraqi described how and why he stabbed to death and set fire to his wife in the street. He regrets nothing, he said. He had to act in such a way. Because of culture. Because of religion. And because of German politics.

"No," said the slightly-built man before the Munich criminal court, "I don't regret that I killed my wife." He would do it again. She would have earned it. And above all the politics of the Federal Republic of Germany are also guilty of her death. Why: "Because the women here have so many rights, they become immodest."[13]

## Hesha Yones, UK—Hacked to Death

"I understand the panic that parents from some ethnic communities feel in the west's over-sexualised society, but killing your child is a barbaric response," said Yasmin Alibhai-Brown in the *Daily Mail* yesterday. She insisted that there should be no special concession for Abdalla Yones, who began a life sentence on Monday for the murder of his 16-year-old daughter, Heshu. It was the first time in British legal history that a plea of 'honour killing' had been entered. Yones said he stabbed Heshu to death at their west London home, because he feared she was becoming westernised. "She was becoming an independent person," reasoned Alibhai-Brown, one of the consequences of living in the west, which is where Yones, a Kurd, fled the barbaric regime of Saddam Hussein 10 years ago.[14]

## Ibtihaz Hasoun—Israeli Arab

Ibtihaz Hasoun, accused of shaming her family, was recently stabbed to death by her brother, who had summoned villagers to watch him murder his "fallen sister." The villagers celebrated the honor killing. "She married someone outside the village," said one man. "We would do the same thing."[15]

## Fadime Sahindal—Sweden

Fadime Sahindal (1976–2002) was a Kurdish immigrant who moved to Sweden from Turkey at the age of seven. She was murdered by her father, Rahmi, in January 2002 in an "honor killing". BOTKYRKA, Sweden— When Fadime Sahindal told police her life had been threatened, they gave her an alarm system. When she approached politicians for help, they told her to make peace with her parents. And when she appealed in television interviews for aid in escaping a death sentence imposed by her father after she refused an arranged marriage, she provoked sympathy among Swedes—whose more liberal outlook she shared—but little willingness to get involved in a family matter. Now that she's dead, shot in the head by her father, the 26-year-old victim of an "honor killing" is drawing attention to the cultural double standards she battled.[16]

### Noor Almaleki—November 2, 2009

Run over by her Muslim father for being too westernized. She lingered for days.[17]

### Zainab, 19, Her Sister, and Rona Amir Mohammed—Kingston, Ontario

Rona Mohammed, 50, who was found dead in a submerged car on June 30, along with three other female victims: sisters Zainab Shafia, 19, Sahar Shafia, 17, and Geeti Shafia, 13, of Montreal's Saint-Léonard district. The sisters' father, Mohammad Shafia, their mother, Tooba Mohammad Yehya, and their 18-year-old brother, Hamid Mohammad Shafia, have been charged with first-degree murder and conspiracy to commit murder in the four deaths.[18]

### Gulsen P., Germany

Another Muslim girl severely beaten (repeatedly), scared to death of her family (and rightly so), and ultimately brutally murdered because she refused forced Islamic marriage in Turkey. And again a case of brutality of Immigrant shocks the land. The young Turkish woman was beaten to death with a stick, her face unrecognizable, because she loved the wrong man and was pregnant with his child.[19]

### Aasiya Hassan

A beheading in Buffalo: Muzzammil Hassan, a prominent Muslim American businessman in Buffalo, New York, is charged with beheading his estranged wife, Aasiya Hassan, in which some suggest is an "honor killing."[20]

### Sandeela Kanwal

Sandeela Kanwal, 25, was found dead on her bedroom floor last July. Her father told police he strangled his daughter with a bungee cord because she wanted a divorce. When she was just 19, Sandeela Kanwal traveled from America to Pakistan for an arranged marriage to a cousin twice her age. Less than six years later, she was dead—strangled—and her father, Chaudhry Rashid, was arrested by police as the suspect for what some have called an "honor killing."[21]

### Morsal Obeidi

At age 16, all Morsal Obeidi wanted was to live the way other girls in Germany do. She paid dearly: Obeidi's brother stabbed her 20 times. Her murder has sparked a renewed debate in Germany about the failure of many immigrant families to integrate into Western society.[22]

### Pela Atroshi—Honor Killing

Mortally wounded and bleeding profusely, Pela Atroshi covered her head with her hands, pleading "please don't shoot me, please don't shoot me". As her sister and her mother screamed, her uncle Rezkar Atroshi raised his gun and killed her. The family's honour had been cleansed.

Rezkar had already shot Pela twice in the back in the upstairs room. Helped downstairs by her mother and her younger sister, the 19-year-old Kurdish Swede was confronted by four resolute men - her father and his three brothers. The men pulled the women apart. Her youngest uncle then finished the job, shooting Pela in the head. The bullet went through one of her fingers and into her brain. The decision to kill her was made by a council of male relatives, led by Pela's grandfather, Abdulmajid Atroshi — a Kurd who lived in Australia.

One of his sons, Shivan Atroshi, helped pull the women away from Pela so his younger brother could get a clean shot. Shivan, too, lived in Australia.

It is the first time an officially confirmed honour killing with a connection to Australia has ever publicly come to light, but it is likely there have been other Australian-connected honour crimes that have been kept hidden within the tight-lipped Australian Kurdish community.[23]

### Uzma Rahan, 32, and Sons, Adam, 11, and Abbas, 8, and 6-Year-Old Daughter Henna

A taxi driver was today jailed for life for bludgeoning his wife and three children to death with a rounders bat over her affair with a married man. Rahan Arshad, 36, committed the murders and then fled on a pre-booked flight to Thailand, leaving the bodies to remain undiscovered in the family home at Cheadle Hulme, Greater Manchester, for almost a month.[24]

### Ten Women Beheaded in Iraq

The images in the Basra police file are nauseating: Page after page of women killed in brutal fashion—some strangled to death, their faces disfigured; others beheaded. All bear signs of torture. The women are killed, police say, because they failed to wear a headscarf or because they ignored other "rules" that secretive fundamentalist groups want to enforce. "Fear, fear is always there," says 30-year-old Safana, an artist and university professor. "We don't know who to be afraid of. Maybe it's a friend or a student you teach. There is no break, no security. I don't know who to be afraid of." Her fear is justified. Iraq's second-largest city, Basra, is a stronghold of conservative Shia groups. As many as 133 women were killed in Basra last year—79 for violation of "Islamic teachings" and 47 for so-called honor killings, according to IRIN, the news branch of the U.N.'s Office for the Coordination of Humanitarian Affairs. One glance through the police file is enough to understand the consequences. Basra's police chief, Gen. Abdul Jalil Khalaf, flips through the file, pointing to one unsolved case after another.[25]

## Samaira Nazir, UK

Azhar Nazir, 30, and his cousin, 17, used four knives to cut Samaira Nazir's throat and repeatedly stab her after she fell in love with an asylum-seeker from what they saw as an unsuitable caste.[26]

## Hina Saleem, Italy

Mohammed Saleem cut his daughter's throat because she refused an arranged marriage and instead wanted to integrate into Italian society.[27]

## Aqsa Parvez, Canada

Aqsa Parvez lies in an unmarked grave despite our efforts to right that terrible wrong. What could be worse for a child living in fear of getting killed by her/his parents? Aqsa Parvez, 16, died Monday, December 10, 2007, a night after being attacked in her home by her father. Aqsa was killed by her father for refusing to follow her family's tradition.[28]

## Caneze Riaz, 39, and Her Four Daughters: Sayrah, 16, Sophia, 15, Alicia, 10, and Hannah, 3, UK

Mohammed Riaz made every conceivable attempt to prevent his wife and daughters enjoying their Westernised lifestyle. He destroyed their clothes—modest by Western standards but tight fitting by his own—when they came out of the wash and he railed against plans to allow alcohol at his terminally ill son's 18th birthday party—which had been brought forward because of his prognosis. Increasingly alienated and in despair over the illness of his son, Adam, the labourer killed his wife and four daughters by throwing petrol over them as they slept and igniting it.[29]

### Dua Khalil, 17, Iraq

A 17-year-old girl has been stoned to death in Iraq because she loved a teenage boy of the wrong religion. As a horrifying video of the stoning went out on the Internet, the British arm of Amnesty International condemned the death of Dua Khalil Aswad as "an abhorrent murder" and demanded that her killers be brought to justice. Reports from Iraq said a local security force witnessed the incident, but did nothing to try to stop it. Now her boyfriend is in hiding in fear for his life.[30]

### Abu Ghanem, 19

Dr. Suliman Abu Ghanem, a 33-year-old pediatrician at Assag Harofeh Hospital, along with his three brother's decided to murder his sister for refusing an arranged marriage. In an indictment submitted to the Tel Aviv District Court Tuesday, four brothers were charged with murdering their sister in an "honor killing." According to the indictment, it was Dr. Suliman Abu Ghanem, a 33-year-old pediatrician at Assaf Harofeh Hospital, who decided to murder his sister, 19-year-old Rim Abu Ghanem.[31]

### Sabia Rani 19, UK

A teenage bride was beaten to death by her husband while her in-laws who shared the same house ignored her sickening ordeal, a court heard yesterday. Sabia Rani, 19, was repeatedly attacked over a three-week period, suffering bruising over 90 percent of her body and "catastrophic" injuries usually only seen in car crash victims. But not only did four members of her husband's family do nothing to help her, they turned a blind eye as he continued the beatings and ultimately murdered the helpless young woman at the house they all shared, it was alleged. The victim's mother-in-law and a sister-in-law blamed her horrific injuries, which included at least 15 fractures on 10 fractured ribs, on "evil spirits, curses and black magic." Two of the family allegedly lied under oath while giving evidence in husband Shazad Khan's murder trial in a deliberate attempt to help him cheat justice, the court heard.[32]

### The Issue of Slavery

In summer 2008 I spent a week in Ghana, which is one of the countries from which slaves were taken from Africa transported to North America. Generally, people think slavery is strictly an American or European thing, but that is not entirely true. As we looked into the subject of slavery and Islam, we discovered a book called *The Legacy of Arab-Islam in Africa* by John Azumah.

This very interesting and enlightening book discusses a subject that very few people know about. It says that somehow the Islamic world, the Arab world, kept their involvement in slavery a secret.[33]

European-American slavery lasted around three hundred years, and slaves sent to North America made up only a portion of the entire slave trade worldwide. However, Azumah reveals that Islamic slavery has actually lasted 1,400 years, and it still continues in certain parts of the world.[34] Slavery has been practiced through the generations by every Islamic tribe and every group of every Muslim nation. It was by no means a white man's invention.

As we looked into the subject of slavery and studied the true nature of Islam, we learned more about its deception and evil. Millions of people who were enslaved by Muslims and taken through the desert to the Red Sea or the Indian Ocean died. Of those who did survive, most of the men were castrated; if women had any babies, those babies were killed immediately after the birth. Islam is a religion of slavery and oppression, and the depth of its brutality is horrifying. As Christians, we have to stand up and say, "Not anymore!"[35]

The Quran and the Bible cannot be compared on the issue of slavery. The Quran condones the taking of slaves as a type of reward for fighting and for being at war against the unbeliever.

Just the opposite is true in our Bible, the Word of God. It talks about living as a Christian, according to 1 John 3:16: "This is how we know what love is: Jesus Christ laid down his life for us. And we ought to lay down our lives for our brothers."

We learn about the love of God by His sacrificing character, not by the cruel punishment and violence we see in Islam or by their laws. Jesus Christ laid down his life for us. Mohammed came with rules and regulations. He came with punishments for people who do not keep the rules, and people are still punished severely today in parts of the world if they disobey or come against the teaching of Mohammed. Jesus came and died for us. He laid down His life for us, and the Bible says that we also ought to lay down our lives for our brothers. This is the type of relationship we have with God and with one another. It means that we will stand up for the truth—that Jesus is the way and Islam is of the devil.

## The Truth About the Fruit of Islam

When the World Trade Center towers fell in 2001, everyone was shocked. Even though there had been warnings and signs before the attack took place, no one had responded to them. The attack was a wake-up call, and everybody was very upset. The cry of our nation was, "We must do something!" It seemed that America did wake up and was very alert. However, that did not last very long, and we went back to sleep as soon as everything began to return to normal.

Last year we decided to do something to break out of the sleepiness that has fallen over America again. On 9/11, we went out on the streets of Gainesville marching and demonstrating with anti-Islam signs that said things like "Islam is of the devil" and "Stop the Taliban." Other signs said, "Jesus is the only way!" We also had our worship team along and sang and praised God on the streets.

Why did we do that? We received a lot of attention from the TV and news media, and we believe that people needed to know the church is called to stand up and fight for freedom. But more than that, we did it in remembrance of what happened on September 11, 2001, when more than three thousand people were murdered.

Here in America we have freedom of religion, and this is one of the reasons Muslims can practice their faith here without being persecuted. If Islam were only a religion, we could wait until God spoke His judgment on it. However, Islam is not just a religion; it is also a political force. Islamic beliefs completely contradict our Constitution, our American beliefs, our Bible, and our faith. If it would gain control of our nation, it would not hesitate one second to enforce its laws on our society. This is why the church must speak out now against the evil of Islam.

Actually, everyone knows that Islam is a violent and dangerous religion. When the news media interviewed me, they used to ask, "Are you not afraid that something is going to happen to you? Are you not afraid that some type of violent act might be done against you because of your stand?"

And my answer was that yes, we think that might happen. The signs and displays we put in our yard have been vandalized and burned down. We have received life-threatening messages. Those are minor things, but they tell us that more could follow.

If we as the church do not start doing something about the evil of Islam, how will the people in our nation and our world receive help and hope? Fear cannot hold us back. The Bible says in 1 John 4:18 that "perfect love drives out fear." Jesus, who lives in us, conquered the devil, and, as we know by now, Islam is of the devil. Like David, we must take our five stones and put our trust in our God! We have to speak what is right.

Islam is a religion of fear, and many in the Western world have bought into it. Fear is dominating our society, and radical Islam is using it to take over our society. We in the United States must withstand this. We as Christians must stand up against it. This is not Islamophobia or hate speech, as some people like to look at it. We are not preaching hate. Rather, we are examining Christianity, which offers forgiveness through Jesus Christ, and Islam, a religion of brutality.

Psalm 52:3 says, "You love evil rather than good, falsehood rather than speaking the truth." Have we come that far in America? In the many interviews we have done with the news media, the reporters hardly ever really tell the truth. They rarely present our case the way we presented it to them. Rather, they try to candy-coat Islam. We are speaking what is right according to the Word of God. The Bible says there is only one way to God, and that way is Jesus Christ. Our motivation to speak the truth is not based on political correctness or being accepted. We need to get back to the truth and nothing but the truth, so help us God!

The United States of America was founded on the truth and the freedom to declare it. We must get back to the truth, first to the truth of the Bible and second to the truth of experience. We receive e-mails on a regular basis, where people share their experiences with Islam, because they have been overseas and they have seen with their own eyes the Sharia law in practice. If you have experienced something like this, it is no longer a theory you could learn or study at the university. Whether experience or theory, there is no way we can justify Islam at all.

Some Middle Eastern countries, like Saudi Arabia, fund terrorism. The book *Funding Evil* by Dr. Rachel Ehrenfeld reveals that Saudi Arabia, with its billions of dollars, funds terrorist camps and terrorists around the world.[36] This is a country that is dominated by Islam, and we can see the fruit of it. They come to our country, to the Western world, and build mosques all over; it is their right and freedom. Yet, in Saudi Arabia we would not be allowed to build a church. Further, in that country, which is rich, there is a reported 11.6 percent unemployment rate. The estimated number of unreported cases might be even higher.[37] With all of the wealth the nation possesses, its leaders seem not to care about the people. Islam is not a religion of caring and hope.

If you follow the news on a regular basis on what's happening all over the world, many acts of terrorism can be traced back to radical Muslim activity. We are not talking about protests, standing up for rights, or expressing an opinion. We are not talking about an act of war or being at war with someone. We are talking about terrorism, the killing of innocent people.

Muslims have built mosques in our capitol and throughout our country. They have obtained building permits and the services of contractors, and they have been allowed, legally, to do that, without anyone stopping them, without any real persecution, fear of punishment, or death. But if you look at their countries, that would not be true for a Christian organization or church. We would not be allowed to build Christian churches in nations under Islamic rule. If that is how they govern and dominate in their own country, do you believe it would be any different if they begin to control, govern, and dominate in the United States?

Abdul Rahman Al-Sudais is a clergyman appointed by the Saudi Royal family. On June 12th, 2004, he could be found praying for interfaith peace at the East London Mosque in the UK. He said that Muslims should set an example of "the true image of Islam" in their interactions with other communities, "and dispel any misconceptions portrayed in some parts of the media." The history of Islam is the best testament to how different communities can live together in peace and harmony. In his sermons at the Grand Mosque in Makkah, Sudais has condemned deadly terrorist attacks in Saudi Arabia, calling them cowardly and vile.[38]

> Humaid b. 'Abd al-Rahman b. 'Auf reported that his mother Umm Kulthum daughter of 'Uqba b. Abu Mu'ait, and she was one amongst the first emigrants who pledged allegiance to Allah's Apostle (may peace be upon him), as saying that she heard Allah's Messenger (may peace be upon him) as saying: A liar is not one who tries to bring reconciliation amongst people and speaks good (in order to avert dispute), or he conveys good. Ibn Shihab said he did not hear that exemption was granted in anything what the people speak as lie but in three cases: in battle, for bringing reconciliation amongst persons and the narration of the words of the husband to his wife, and the narration of the words of a wife to her husband (in a twisted form in order to bring reconciliation between them).
> —SAHIH MUSLIM BOOK 032, NUMBER 6303

One book of Sharia law called "Reliance of the Traveler" (page 746; 8.2) states:

> Speaking is a means to achieve objectives. If a praiseworthy aim is attainable through both telling the truth and lying, it is unlawful to accomplish through lying because there is no need for it. When it is possible to achieve such an aim by lying but not by telling the truth, it is permissible to lie if attaining the goal is permissible (N:i.e. when the purpose of lying is to circumvent someone who is preventing one from doing something permissible), and obligatory to lie if the goal is obligatory...it is religiously precautionary in all cases to employ words that give a misleading impression.

The Koran allows the Muslim to lie. How can they be trusted with anything they say?

Abdul Rahman Al-Sudais has publicly called the Jews "monkeys and pigs," the "worst of mankind," and "scum of the earth."[39] This is what they really think about unbelievers. How does this fit into living in peace and harmony with the western communities?

In my opinion Muslims do not want to live in peace with other communities. In Dr. Peter Hammond's book *Slavery, Terrorism, and Islam: The Historical Roots and Contemporary Threat*, he talks about how Islamization in a country occurs.[40] If the Muslim population remains around one percent of any given country they will be regarded as a peace-loving minority and not as a threat to anyone.[41]

| Country | Muslim Population |
|---|---|
| United States | 1.0% |
| Australia | 1.5% |
| Canada | 1.9% |
| China | 1% – 2% |
| Italy | 1.5% |
| Norway | 1.8% |

At 2–3 percent they begin to proselytize from other ethnic minorities and disaffected groups with major recruiting from the jails and among street gangs:

| Country | Muslim Population |
|---|---|
| Denmark | 2% |
| Germany | 3.7% |
| United Kingdom | 2.7% |
| Spain | 4% |
| Thailand | 4.6% |

At 5 percent they exercise an excessive influence in proportion to their percentage of the population: pushing for the introduction of halal food (clean by Islamic standards), thereby securing food preparation jobs for Muslims; increasing pressure on supermarket chains to feature it on their shelves; along with threats for failure to comply (United States).

| Country | Muslim Population |
|---|---|
| France | 8% |
| Philippines | 5% |

| | |
|---|---|
| Sweden | 5% |
| Switzerland | 4.3% |
| The Netherlands | 5.5% |
| Trinidad and Tobago | 5.8% |

At this point, they will work to get the ruling government to allow them to rule themselves under Sharia, the Islamic law. The ultimate goal of Islam is not to convert the world but to establish Sharia law over the entire world.

At 10 percent they will increase lawlessness as a means of complaint about their conditions (Paris—car burnings). Any non-Muslim action that offends Islam will result in uprisings and threats (Amsterdam—Mohammed cartoons).

| Country | Muslim Population |
|---|---|
| Guyana | 10% |
| India | 13.4% |
| Israel | 16% |
| Kenya | 10% |
| Russia | 10–15% |

At 20 percent expect hair-trigger rioting, jihad militia formations, sporadic killings, and church and synagogue burning.

| Country | Muslim Population |
|---|---|
| Ethiopia | 32.8% |

At 40 percent expect widespread massacres, chronic terror attacks, and ongoing militia warfare.

| Country | Muslim Population |
|---|---|
| Bosnia | 40% |
| Chad | 53.1% |
| Lebanon | 59.7% |

From 60 percent expect unfettered persecution of non-believers, other religions, sporadic ethnic cleansing, use of Sharia law as a weapon, and Jizya, the tax placed on infidels.

| Country | Muslim Population |
|---|---|
| Albania | 70% |
| Malaysia | 60.4% |
| Qatar | 77.5% |
| Sudan | 70% |

After 80 percent expect state-run ethnic cleansing and genocide.

| Country | Muslim Population |
|---|---|
| Bangladesh | 83% |
| Egypt | 90% |
| Gaza | 98.7% |
| Indonesia | 86.1% |
| Iran | 98% |
| Iraq | 97% |
| Jordan | 92% |
| Morocco | 98.7% |
| Pakistan | 97% |
| Palestine | 99% |
| Syria | 90% |
| Tajikistan | 90% |
| Turkey | 99.8% |
| United Arab Emirates | 96% |

One hundred percent will usher in the peace of "Dar-es-Salaam"—the Islamic House of Peace; there is supposed to be peace because everyone is a Muslim.

| Country | Muslim Population |
|---|---|
| Afghanistan | 100% |
| Saudi Arabia | 100% |
| Somalia | 100% |
| Yemen | 100% |

How can anyone think that Islam is a religion of peace? When we look at the fruit of the approximately fifty-seven Muslim states,[42] we do not see a fruit that we, in the Western world, desire to copy. We do not see democracy and freedom. Rather, we see bondage to Islamic law and the penalty of death for those who convert to another religion. This is not the fruit of peace and tolerance!

# THE VISION OF ISLAM

It is no secret that Islam is growing quickly. The advances it has made through the years and the prognosis for the future can, will, and is about to change the world, if we are not able to do something to counteract it. The danger that comes with Islam is no secret, and leaders in politics and religious systems are well aware of this. Even though the world of Islam is not trying to hide the violent methods by which they rule their nations, the Western world seems to be covered by a garment of denial.

Islam has a plan to take over the world, and although its leaders have no problem proclaiming it, we still are not alarmed. When the two towers fell on 9/11, everybody was talking about how this attack was a wake-up call. However, it seems that no one woke up. And if any did, they must have gone back to sleep right away! We as Christians definitely need a plan, and we must act before it becomes too late. In the United States of America we still might have a chance to stop the development of Islam here. In Europe, Islam is already gaining popularity as a religion, and it is just a matter of time until they take over political control as well. For example, consider the Muslim population in Germany:

> Germany has one of the largest populations of Muslim immigrants in Western Europe, with a Muslim community of over 3 million. That trend is expected to continue, leading some demographic trend-watchers to warn that the country is well on the way to becoming a Muslim state by 2050, *Deutsche Welle* reported.
>
> *The Brussels Journal* reported last month that one third of all European children will be born to Muslim families by 2025. There are an estimated 50 million Muslims living in Europe today—that number is expected to double over the next twenty years.[1]

I lived in Germany for more than thirty years, and I have seen this development with my own eyes. My wife is German; she grew up there. Together we feel very strongly that the development is not healthy and positive. This is why we are writing this book and calling the church to action. We put our hope in God that if the church takes their stand and position, there is still hope. If not, we are convinced the future is like the Bible prophecies, very, very dark! The purpose of this book is not to pass along facts, but rather to call the church back to biblical faith and action so God can bless the nations and us!

The war on terrorism is overrated. We are fighting the wrong war, and it is a distraction. It is not even necessary anymore; however, Islam is taking over in the areas that we, the church, are ignoring:

- the advancement of its message
- the radicalness of its evangelism
- its birthrate

Muammar al-Gaddafi said, "There are signs that Allah will grant Islam victory in Europe—without swords, without guns, without conquests. The 50 million Muslims of Europe will turn it into a Muslim continent within a few decades."[2]

In 1970 100,000 Muslims were living in the United States. In 2008 that number had grown to 9 million. In the next few years 50 million Muslims will be living here. As you can see, the prognosis for the United States does not look a whole lot better than it does for Europe. We must wake up. The Catholic Church has admitted that for the first time in history the population of the Muslim believers has surpassed that of the Catholic believers. With their increasing growth it is indeed possible that Islam will, in the next five to seven years, become the dominant religion in the world.

Instead of stopping this development, we are causing and supporting the advancement of Islam through:

- Watering down the pure gospel from the message that "Jesus is the only way to eternal life with God" to "We all have the same God somehow."
- The decline of evangelism from the Western world and the sending of missionaries mainly to South America, Africa, or Asia.
- Abortion, the killing of thousands of lives each day.
- Approving homosexuality and same sex marriage in the modern Christian church.

How could this happen, and what can we do? If you search YouTube, you will quickly learn that the Islamic message is dominating there. You will see testimonies and Islam's plans to evangelize America through the media and politics. The Islamic world proclaims aloud that it not only wants Israel or the

U.S., but it also wants the world.[3] If it cannot take the world by force, it will take it by marriage. When I traveled and spoke in places in Africa, people told me that it is very common among the Muslims to proselytize with slogans like "Christianity gives you one wife; Islam gives you four!"

> Marry women of your choice, Two or three or four…
> —Quran Surah 4:3, Yusuf Ali Translation

The Bible allows one wife:

> For this reason a man will leave his father and mother and be united to his wife, and they will become one flesh.
> —Genesis 2:24

> An elder must be blameless, the husband of but one wife.
> —Titus 1:6

## A Vision to Take Over the World

The vision of Islam is to take over the world. It has a plan, and its members are willing to pay any price to fulfill it. They are not worried about what other people might say, and they are definitely not shy about expressing their radical message. Omar Ahmad, the founder of CAIR (The Council of American-Islamic Relations), reportedly said in the late nineties, "Islam isn't in America to be equal to any other faith, but to become dominant. The Koran, the Muslim book of scripture, should be the highest authority in America, and Islam the only accepted religion on Earth."[4]

The vision of radical Muslims—their mission—is to convert the world to Islamic law and make church and state one. They are part of a political system like communism, where a few in power promise a better life. They have declared jihad, holy war, on the world, and they are waging it in three ways:

1. Through the brutal and violent war of terror and punishment.
2. Through cultural war. They are not interested in integrating into our society. They are interested in changing our Christian culture. They want us to act like them, dress like them, and obey their laws.
3. Though financial jihad. Their money and finances enable them to fulfill their vision.

Freedom House, a watchdog organization that does spot checks on mosques and their activities, checked out the literature of over two hundred mosques in major cities including Dallas, Houston, Chicago, New York, Washington,

DC, Los Angeles, and Oakland. In these mosques, they discovered a couple hundred books that were published and paid for by Saudi Arabia. These books express the vision of Islam by telling Muslims how to deal with unbelievers.[5]

One of the statements in these books is, "Hate them for their religion." Islam is a religion of peace only to the people who have not studied it. These books use the word *hate* many times. In a direct quote, they say, "In dealing with infidels [people like us], hate them for their religion."[6] They indoctrinate their little children from a very young age and teach them how to hate. They state, "Hate them for Allah's sake, and oppose them in every way. Build up a wall of resistance against them."

The Internet is flooded with information on how intensely they teach their children to hate all "non-believers." For example, they have programs in their services or ceremonies where the children act out plays and games of massacre, dressed like suicide bombers, holding toy machineguns with hands colored red, like blood.[7] Compare this to our Sunday school material on stories such as those about Noah's ark and David and Goliath. Radical Islam is teaching its children to hate everyone else for their religion.

In response to the instruction of the aforementioned literature to "oppose them in every way," radical Muslims are not trying to be a part of the great melting pot society here in America. Rather, because of their vision for world domination, they are opposing the society. They put up a wall of resistance with the goal of conquering and then destroying Western society.

These books say that democracy is responsible for all of the world's problems, and the radical Muslims within the borders of our free land act on these words by opposing democracy, justice, brotherhood, and equality. Their vision is dictatorship under brutal Islamic laws—rules and regulations that give no mercy. This is a far cry from what we want to welcome into our nation, a far cry from the foundation of our nation, a far cry from Jesus and His message of love and forgiveness.

Islam wants to take away our First Amendment rights. Europeans have already lost most of their freedom to laws that stop people from speaking the truth. For example, Dutch filmmaker Geert Wilders dared to make a film that criticizes Islam, and he is being prosecuted. He may wind up in prison for stating his opinion.[8] This is an example of the way other countries have limited the freedom of speech by playing with words. If you say anything that is a little controversial, it is not only labeled as hate but is also declared to be against the law and considered punishable. We must protect our First Amendment and make people aware of what is going on in our world.

The vision of radical Islamic law is a call for the death of all unbelievers, including Christians. If this vision is fulfilled, Muslims themselves are executed if they fail to live under Islamic law. And, Islam is the number one enemy of Israel. Its desire is for all of the Jews throughout the world to be destroyed. In 2006 the Iranian President said, "I therefore declare that this sinister regime, Israel, is the banner of Satan, it is the great banner of Satan." At the end of the speech, he was joined by the crowd as he cried, "Death to Israel, Death to Israel, Death to Israel."[9] The same president is not only proclaiming this about Israel, but about America as well![10] We as Christians must stand up against the evil of Islam. God said that He will bless us if we will bless Israel, pray for Israel, and show its people that Jesus Christ is the true Messiah.

## A Vision That We Must Fight

Islam, a dangerous religion and political force, is indeed a demonic system. It has made much headway in our generation, especially into Europe, and now it is creeping into the United States. It is a powerful demonic force and we as Christians are standing by and letting it happen. It will take over the world if we remain silent. However, we serve a living, merciful, and powerful God who is more powerful than Islam or any other force. If we will stand up and oppose the advancement of Islam, He will manifest His power through us.

The problem we have with Islamic growth is simply the fact that the church is not present Almost no church or Christian stands up for the truth in a firm and clear way, declaring that Jesus Christ, the Son of God, is the only way to salvation. The church is not radical anymore, and to return to the radical message of the gospel, we must start a new war. The Bible says in Ephesians 6 that we are not fighting against flesh and blood but against the powers of darkness. Look at how we are to fight the powers of evil:

> Put on the full armor of God so that you can take your stand against the devil's schemes. For our struggle is not against flesh and blood, but against the rulers, against the authorities, against the powers of this dark world and against the spiritual forces of evil in the heavenly realms. Therefore put on the full armor of God, so that when the day of evil comes, you may be able to stand your ground, and after you have done everything, to stand. Stand firm then, with the belt of truth buckled around your waist, with the breastplate of righteousness in place, and with your feet fitted with the readiness that comes from the gospel of peace. In addition to all this, take up the shield of faith, with which you can extinguish all the flaming arrows of the evil one. Take the helmet of salvation and the

sword of the Spirit, which is the word of God. And pray in the Spirit on all occasions with all kinds of prayers and requests. With this in mind, be alert and always keep on praying for all the saints.
—Ephesians 6:11–18

We must start a spiritual war against the lukewarmness in the body of Christ. This starts with prayer, but it must be followed by steps that produce action. In other words, we have to bring balance to the force!

The vision—the mission—of Islam is world control, world domination. As Christians, we have the mission of world salvation. Our mission is that all people—homosexuals, adulterers, fornicators, as well as Muslims—would come to the knowledge of Jesus Christ and His saving power. But we see Christians backing off in our world. We see them hiding in the mountains like the children of Israel (1 Sam. 17:8–11, 24). We must call out the Davids; we must call out the church. Islam is waging jihad, holy war, and we as Christians are fighting a holy war too. We are not killing people as they are, but we are indeed in a battle for the minds and the souls of people.

The United States started the war against terrorism after we lost around three thousand lives in the 9/11 tragedy. We lose more babies than that by abortion every day in the United States, and we just take it.[11] We must stand up against gay marriages and return to Christian family traditions.

We must rearrange our priorities. As Christians we must wake up and stop all the things that occupy our time, whether they be Christian activities or hobbies; we must make it our focus to evangelize and preach the gospel. We need to get out on the street and speak the message of truth. We cannot look at the world and flow with them. We must look to the Bible and create our own flow. Instead of having conferences about prophetic dreams and visions or making a better life, we must wake up and mobilize the Christian community to evangelize. We must become radical in this area.

As you can easily see, I used the word *must* many times in the preceding paragraphs. The Bible says that you must believe in Jesus Christ, the Son of God, to get saved. If you talk to people this way, they often accuse you of being controlling, judgmental, or legalistic. This is exactly the reason Christians do not evangelize anymore. They are afraid of being accused, rejected, and persecuted. Jesus said that we can expect this.

> Remember the words I spoke to you: "No servant is greater than his master." If they persecuted me, they will persecute you also. If they obeyed my teaching, they will obey yours also.
> —John 15:20

## The Folly of Self-Delusion

We found that almost all the churches we contacted in our city, and many Christians we talked to on the streets in our daily outreaches in our area, agreed with the Bible that homosexuality is not an "alternative" lifestyle but an ungodly lifestyle. It is a lifestyle that, like fornication, adultery, and abortion, has become accepted in our society, even though it is wrong.

Recently there was a gay pride march in our city, and our church decided to do an outreach there. Before the march, we contacted 120 churches about working with us, and to our great, great shame as Christians, out of all the people we contacted and of all the people who agreed with us, no one showed up. As we went to the march and reached out to meet the homosexuals and offer them real life—the real life in Jesus—we were not even allowed on the square where the gay pride parade was held. Why? Because they had rented it. As Christians, God's children, presenting the message of life in Jesus Christ, we were not allowed in the town square, simply because of money. We in the kingdom of God must be creative. We must not only make money so that we can have a better lifestyle, but also because money means influence, power, and control. If we don't have it, the opponents of the truth will! And they don't hesitate to spend it!

We reach out to homosexuals to offer them the true life in Jesus. Do you know what Islam offers them? Islam's offer to homosexuals is execution; it is death. They simply kill the homosexual, along with all unbelievers. All homosexuals should actually be on our side because we are fighting for their lives!

When we look at Islamic nations, what do we see? We see countries that are ruled by Islamic law and the violence that happens in those places. We see Saudi Arabia, Iran, and Sudan. We see groups like the Taliban and Al-Qaeda.

We live in a dangerous time, a very explosive time. We must wake up and look at what is going on in the world. Islam, a violent and oppressive political system, is at work in Western culture, even though it may seem passive. For example, 10 percent of the two thousand mosques in the United States are preaching jihad, as it is based on the Quran.[12] Yes, and we must heed the words Ronald Reagan spoke at the House of Parliament in England in 1982. He said, "Self-delusion in the face of unpleasant facts is folly."[13]

As Christians, we are sticking our heads in the sand in self-delusion. We are hiding. We are not willing to stand up. We are more interested in programs and in pleasing people than we are in pleasing God. How blind are we in America? How blind are our churches? How blind are our politicians to think we can just close our eyes and this evil thing will go away?

We have a message of salvation. You need to be saved, and Jesus is the only way to forgiveness, life, eternal life, and salvation. Islam does not offer the power of salvation. If you examine Christianity and Islam, you see that Christianity is mainly a religion of love and peace. It is a message of people being reunited with God through Jesus Christ. However, if you look at Islam and the nations that are controlled by Islam, you see the rule of brutality and force that it envisions.

# The SPIRIT of the ANTICHRIST  6

*How long will mockers delight in mockery and fools hate knowledge?*
—Proverbs 1:22

*Do not rebuke a mocker or he will hate you; rebuke a wise man and he will love you.*
—Proverbs 9:8

THE SEARCHING QUESTION OF PROVERBS 1:22 applies to the people who send us e-mails arrogantly making fun of the Bible. It also speaks to us as Christians and asks if we are going to live as fools by closing our eyes to knowledge and to the developments in the world around us. We take our freedom for granted, and too often the body of Christ looks like a big clown playing church as the mockers have their fun. Rather than living as fools, we must seek to know the truth and receive any rebuke, as Proverbs 9:8 describes it, that will lead us to it.

A wise man is a person who wants to know the truth. Such a person asks, Is the Bible true? Is Islam really something we must stand up against? Is Islam the end-time Antichrist? Even with the threat of Islam in our world today, many Christians do not ask these questions but rather choose to compromise. They forget that God is a jealous God and that you cannot serve two masters.

In his book *The Islamic Antichrist*, Joel Richardson explains that choosing to compromise is rejecting God. He defines *compromise* as "the action of building bridges to Islam," because most of the Muslims we may know are nice and peaceful and also believe that Jesus is coming back. He explains that these "nice and peaceful" Muslims do believe Jesus is coming back, but their Jesus is a Muslim Jesus who will destroy Christianity.[1]

As we face the Islamic threat, we must repent of compromise in our lives, because we need to know that our God is fighting on our side as Christians. We must come back to God with a true heart. Joel 2:12–14 says:

But there's also this, it's not too late—God's personal Message!—"Come back to me and really mean it! Come fasting and weeping, sorry for your sins!" Change your life, not just your clothes. Come back to God, your God. And here's why: God is kind and merciful. He takes a deep breath, puts up with a lot, This most patient God, extravagant in love, always ready to cancel catastrophe. Who knows? Maybe he'll do it now, maybe he'll turn around and show pity. Maybe, when all's said and done, there'll be blessings full and robust for your God! (THE MESSAGE)

When we repent and declare the challenge God gives us, His provision of forgiveness is revealed and His plans of punishment and destruction can be changed into blessing. This is what the prophet Jonah declared after he went to Nineveh and preached. He said in Jonah 4:2:

> I knew that you are a gracious and compassionate God, slow to anger and abounding in love, a God who relents from sending calamity.

The Word of God has many scriptures that speak about the End Times and the Antichrist. This chapter is not intended to give you a theological or precise analysis of all these scriptures and what they could mean. And I have no ambitions to give any kind of proof that Islam is the Antichrist, even though no other religion would fit better into this role. Instead, I want to take us to the teaching the apostle John gave concerning the spirit of the Antichrist.

> This is how you can recognize the Spirit of God: Every spirit that acknowledges that Jesus Christ has come in the flesh is from God, but every spirit that does not acknowledge Jesus is not from God. This is the spirit of the antichrist, which you have heard is coming and even now is already in the world.
>
> —1 JOHN 4:2–3

When John wrote this, he recognized that the spirit of the Antichrist was already in the world. Nevertheless, Christians through the centuries have been able to follow Jesus. The spirit of the Antichrist is in the world today, and we have become very used to it. The lukewarmness of the church gives proof to that! The main question for us is not, Who is the person of the Antichrist and how can we be protected from him? The real question is, Who is denying that Jesus Christ is the Son of God who has come in the flesh?

The remainder of this chapter will show what Islam teaches about Jesus and then provide biblical truth concerning Christ and the triune God. It will very clearly confirm that Islam is indeed of the devil!

# The Quran Says...

## The denial of Jesus, the Son of God

The Quran completely denies the Sonship of Christ, the fact that Jesus died on the cross for our sins, and the Trinity as well.

> In blasphemy are those indeed who say that God is Christ, the son of Mary.
> —Surah 5:17, Yusuf Ali Translation

> Christians call Christ the son of Allah that is a saying from their mouth, they but imitate what the unbelievers of old used to say. Allah's curse be on them: how they are deluded away from the truth.
> —Surah 9:30, Yusuf Ali Translation

> That they say they killed Christ Jesus the son of Mary, the messenger of Allah; but they killed him not, nor crucified him, but so it was made to appear to them and those who differ therein are full of doubts with no knowledge, but only conjecture to follow, for of a surety they killed him not: Nay, Allah raised him up unto himself; and Allah is exalted in power, wise.
> —Surah 4:157–158, Yusuf Ali Translation

> They do blaspheme who say Allah is one of three in a trinity for there is no God except one Allah. If they desist not from their word (of blasphemy), verily a grievous penalty will befall the blasphemers among them.
> —Surah 5:73, Yusuf Ali Translation

## The Mahdi

To the Muslims, Jesus is a prophet only and not the Son of God. Nevertheless, He has an important part in the End Times. They believe, like the Christians, that Jesus will come back to Earth but not as a Savior or Messiah. Islam's messiah is called the Mahdi, and they await him just like we Christians await Jesus, the Soon-coming King, to bring justice to the world. The Mahdi will be their ruler of the world.

> After the lesser signs of the hour appear and increase, mankind will have reached a stage of great suffering, then the awaited Mahdi will appear. He is the first of the greater clear signs of the hour.
> —Kabbani, Approach of Armageddon, 228

> The Mahdi will establish right and justice to the world and eliminate evil and corruption. He will fight against the enemies who would be victorious.

He will reappear on the appointing day, and then he will fight against the forces of evil, lead a world revolution, and set up a new world order based on justice, righteousness and virtue—ultimately the righteous will take the world administration in their hands and Islam will be victorious over all the religions.

He is the precursor of the victory of the truth and the fall of all tyrants. He heralds the end of injustice and oppression and the beginning of the final rising of the sun of Islam which will never again set and which will ensure happiness and the elevation of mankind. The Mahdi is one of Allah's clear signs which will soon be made evident to everyone.[2]

—Abdulaziz, Abdulhussein, and Sachedina, *Islamic Messianism*

In Islam, Jesus has an inferior position compared to the Mahdi. Their Jesus will follow the Mahdi and teaches the Muslims according to the Quran. They believe Christians will convert to Islam and reject the fact that He would be the Son of God.

At this very time Allah would send Christ, son of Mary, and he will descend at the white minaret in the eastern side of Damascus wearing two garments lightly dyed with saffron and placing his hands on the wings of two angels.[3]

—Sahih Muslim Book 041, Number 7015

Muslims will still be preparing themselves for the battle drawing up the ranks. Certainly, the time of prayer shall come and then Jesus, son of Mary, would descend.[4]

—Veliankode, *Doomsday: portents and prophesies*

Jesus will come and will perform the obligatory prayers behind the Mahdi and follow him. Jesus will be following the Mahdi, the master of all time and that is why he will be offering his prayers behind him.[5]

—Sahih Muslim Book 001, Number 0293

Jesus, the son of Mary will descend and will lead them judging amongst them according to the holy Qur'an and the Sunnah of the prophet Muhammad.[6]

—Al-Sadr and Mutahhar, *the awaited Saviour*

There is not one of the people of the scripture (Christians and Jews) but will believe in him before his death, and on the day of resurrection he will be a witness against them.

—Surah 4:159

Jesus will descend from heaven and espouse the cause of the Mahdi. The Christians and the Jews will see him and recognize his true status. The Christians will abandon their faith in his Godhead.[7]

—Shafi, Kashmiri, Usmani, and Rehman
*Signs of the Qiyamah and the Arrival of the Maseeh*

### The sin of shirk

The greatest sin and crime to a Muslim is the sin of *shirk*, to believe in any other God than Allah.[8] There is no greater crime in the Islamic world that you can admit than *shirk*. Muslims consider "the oneness of Allah," called the doctrine of Tawhid, to be absolute. They profess that Allah is one and alone. In the eye of Islam, Christianity is the number one lawbreaker of their most important commandment, which must be enforced under all circumstances.

## The Bible Says…

### Jesus is the Son of God

> For God so loved the world that he gave his one and only Son, that whoever believes in him shall not perish but have eternal life.
> —John 3:16

> This is how God showed his love among us: He sent his one and only Son into the world that we might live through him.
> —1 John 4:9

> For I have come down from heaven not to do my will but to do the will of him who sent me. And this is the will of him who sent me, that I shall lose none of all that he has given me, but raise them up at the last day. For my Father's will is that everyone who looks to the Son and believes in him shall have eternal life, and I will raise him up at the last day.
> —John 6:38–40

The Bible calls everyone who denies that Jesus has come in the flesh as the Son of God an Antichrist. The Antichrist is first of all a deceiving spirit that lies with no limits.

> Who is the liar? It is the man who denies that Jesus is the Christ. Such a man is the antichrist—he denies the Father and the Son. No one who denies the Son has the Father; whoever acknowledges the Son has the Father also.
> —1 John 2:22

> Many deceivers, who do not acknowledge Jesus Christ as coming in the flesh, have gone out into the world. Any such person is the deceiver and the antichrist.
>
> —2 John 1:7

## The Word became flesh

Jesus is the spoken Word of God, who became flesh to save us from our sin and to reunite us with God the Father.

> In the beginning was the Word, and the Word was with God, and the Word was God. He was with God in the beginning. Through him all things were made; without him nothing was made that has been made. In him was life, and that life was the light of men. The light shines in the darkness, but the darkness has not understood it. There came a man who was sent from God; his name was John. He came as a witness to testify concerning that light, so that through him all men might believe. He himself was not the light; he came only as a witness to the light. The true light that gives light to every man was coming into the world. He was in the world, and though the world was made through him, the world did not recognize him. He came to that which was his own, but his own did not receive him. Yet to all who received him, to those who believed in his name, he gave the right to become children of God—children born not of natural descent, nor of human decision or a husband's will, but born of God. The Word became flesh and made his dwelling among us. We have seen his glory, the glory of the One and Only, who came from the Father, full of grace and truth.
>
> —John 1:1–14

## The Cross

Jesus died on the cross for our sins and was resurrected on the third day. The Crucifixion and, of course, the Resurrection are the central points of Christianity! Without the sacrifice of Jesus there would be no salvation and eternal life with God, but eternal life in hell; and, the Bible would just be another religious book of rules and regulations. The concept of sacrifice is what we have lost in the Western Christian society, and this is why the church is weak. There is resurrection power in this sacrifice that destroyed the devil's powers, including the power of Islam. Because of the Crucifixion there is hope for us!

> Christ redeemed us from that self-defeating, cursed life by absorbing it completely into himself. Do you remember the Scripture that says, "Cursed is everyone who hangs on a tree"? That is what happened when Jesus was nailed to the cross: He became a curse, and at the same time

dissolved the curse. And now, because of that, the air is cleared and we can see that Abraham's blessing is present and available for non-Jews, too. We are all able to receive God's life, his Spirit, in and with us by believing—just the way **Abraham** received it.
—Galatians 3:13–14, the message

In putting everything under him, God left nothing that is not subject to him. Yet at present we do not see everything subject to him. But we see Jesus, who was made a little **lower than** the angels, now crowned with glory and honor because he **suffered** death, so that by the grace of God he might taste death for everyone. In bringing many sons to glory, it was fitting that God, for whom and through whom everything exists, should make the author of their salvation perfect through suffering.
—Hebrews 2:8–10

Unlike the other high priests, he does not need to offer sacrifices day after day, first for his own sins, and then for the sins of the people. He sacrificed for their sins once for all when he offered himself.
—Hebrews 7:27

And by that will, we have been made holy through the sacrifice of the body of Jesus Christ once for all.
—Hebrews 10:10

Therefore, brothers, since we have confidence to enter the Most Holy Place by the blood of Jesus, by a new and living way opened for us through the curtain, that is, his body, and since we have a great priest over the house of God, let us draw near to God with a sincere heart in full assurance of faith, having our hearts sprinkled to cleanse us from a guilty conscience and having our bodies washed with pure water.
—Hebrews 10:19–22

Therefore, since we are surrounded by such a great cloud of witnesses, let us throw off everything that hinders and the sin that so easily entangles, and let us run with perseverance the race marked out for us. Let us fix our eyes on Jesus, the author and perfecter of our faith, who for the joy set before him endured the cross, scorning its shame, and sat down at the right hand of the throne of God.
—Hebrews 12:1–2

The altar from which God gives us the gift of himself is not for exploitation by insiders who grab and loot. In the old system, the animals are killed and the bodies disposed of outside the camp. The blood is then brought inside to the altar as a sacrifice for sin. It's the same with Jesus.

He was crucified outside the city gates—that is where he poured out the sacrificial blood that was brought to God's altar to cleanse his people.
—Hebrews 13:10–12, the message

This is the kind of life you've been invited into, the kind of life Christ lived. He suffered everything that came his way so you would know that it could be done, and also know how to do it, step-by-step. He never did one thing wrong, Not once said anything amiss. They called him every name in the book and he said nothing back. He suffered in silence, content to let God set things right. He used his servant body to carry our sins to the Cross so we could be rid of sin, free to live the right way. His wounds became your healing. You were lost sheep with no idea who you were or where you were going. Now you're named and kept for good by the Shepherd of your souls.
—1 Peter 2:21–25, the message

**The Trinity**

God-Father, God-Son, and God-Holy Spirit. Jesus is the spoken Word of God who became flesh and came to Earth. After dying on the cross, Jesus was put into the grave. On the third day the Father resurrected Jesus from the dead through the power of His Holy Spirit. After a time of appearing to His disciples, Jesus returned to heaven, but He did not leave us alone. He sent the Holy Spirit of the Father to the Earth. The Holy Spirit is the part of God that is working with us here on Earth. Saved through the blood of Jesus and filled with the power of the Holy Spirit, we are able and called to fulfill the will of God, to overcome evil, and to build God's kingdom here on Earth, like it is in heaven.

*The Beginning: God and the Holy Spirit*

In the beginning God created the heavens and the earth. Now the earth was formless and empty, darkness was over the surface of the deep, and the Spirit of God was hovering over the waters.
—Genesis 1:1–2

*The Word Became Flesh: God and Jesus*

In the beginning was the Word, and the Word was with God, and the Word was God. He was with God in the beginning.
—John 1:1–2

*Recognize the Spirit of God*

This is how you can recognize the Spirit of God: Every spirit that acknowledges that Jesus Christ has come in the flesh is from God, but every spirit that does not acknowledge Jesus is not from God. This is the spirit of the antichrist, which you have heard is coming and even now is already in the world.

—1 John 4:2–3

*Inseparable Unity of the Trinity*

This is the one who came by water and blood—Jesus Christ. He did not come by water only, but by water and blood. And it is the Spirit who testifies, because the Spirit is the truth. For there are three that testify: the Spirit, the water and the blood; and the three are in agreement. We accept man's testimony, but God's testimony is greater because it is the testimony of God, which he has given about his Son. Anyone who believes in the Son of God has this testimony in his heart. Anyone who does not believe God has made him out to be a liar, because he has not believed the testimony God has given about his Son. And this is the testimony: God has given us eternal life, and this life is in his Son. He who has the Son has life; he who does not have the Son of God does not have life. I write these things to you who believe in the name of the Son of God so that you may know that you have eternal life.

—1 John 5:6–13

*God's Confirmation*

Jesus replied, "Let it be so now; it is proper for us to do this to fulfill all righteousness." Then John consented. As soon as Jesus was baptized, he went up out of the water. At that moment heaven was opened, and he saw the Spirit of God descending like a dove and lighting on him. And a voice from heaven said, "This is my Son, whom I love; with him I am well pleased."

—Matthew 3:15–17

*The Gift of the Holy Spirit*

Peter replied, "Repent and be baptized, every one of you, in the name of Jesus Christ for the forgiveness of your sins. And you will receive the gift of the Holy Spirit."

—Acts 2:38

This Jesus, God raised up. And every one of us here is a witness to it. Then, raised to the heights at the right hand of God and receiving the promise of the Holy Spirit from the Father, he poured out the Spirit he had just received. That is what you see and hear.

—Acts 2:33, the message

He went on to open their understanding of the Word of God, showing them how to read their Bibles this way. He said, "You can see now how it is written that the Messiah suffers, rises from the dead on the third day, and then a total life-change through the forgiveness of sins is proclaimed in his name to all nations—starting from here, from Jerusalem! You're the first to hear and see it. You're the witnesses. What comes next is very important: I am sending what my Father promised to you, so stay here in the city until he arrives, until you're equipped with power from on high." He then led them out of the city over to Bethany. Raising his hands he blessed them, and while blessing them, took his leave, being carried up to heaven.

—Luke 24:45–51, the message

# WHAT WOULD JESUS SAY ABOUT ISLAM?

WHEN OUR CHURCH, DOVE WORLD Outreach Center, put up a sign that said, "Islam is of the devil," we received national and international attention. We have done TV and radio interviews, and one day we had twenty-one thousand hits on our Web site. Our stand for truth has stirred many people to either positive or negative reactions.

As you think about your response to our sign, I would like to remind you of something Christians typically do when they are faced with difficult questions about a particular course of action. They often ask, "Would Jesus do this?" I think we can ask this question about the statement that Islam is of the devil. Would Jesus say that? In this chapter, we will see that the Bible is quite clear about what is of the devil.

## Betrayers Are of the Devil

One of Jesus' twelve disciples, His closest companions during His earthly ministry, was called a devil. In John 6:70–71 Jesus said:

> Jesus answered them, Did I not choose you, the Twelve? And [yet] one of you is a devil (of the evil one and a false accuser). He was speaking of Judas, the son of Simon Iscariot, for he was about to betray Him, [although] he was one of the Twelve. (AMP)

Jesus Himself chose His twelve disciples, and still the devil's nature was found in them. Being a disciple, a pastor, a Christian, or a member of a famous ministry does not make us OK. Rather, it is our loyalty to the kingdom of God and His vision and call (plans) for us as the church. Judas, one of the disciples, was with Jesus every day, but he did not understand a bit of the mission Jesus came to accomplish. As soon as Jesus' way turned away from Judas's imaginations, Judas became a betrayer.

I have seen this phenomenon many, many times in my ministry. People swear and proclaim that God put them beside you and that they will always be there with you. However, as soon as something goes differently than they wanted it to be, they turn their back on you. The closer they are to you, the greater the damage they produce. According to the Bible, a betrayer is of the devil. Jesus said it Himself. And if Jesus says that something is of the devil, we have to follow His example and call the same things by the same name!

## Sinners Are of the Devil

> He who does what is sinful is of the devil, because the devil has been sinning from the beginning. The reason the Son of God appeared was to destroy the devil's work.
>
> —1 John 3:8

In this verse, the Bible says that the person who commits sin is of the devil. Each time we sin, we are of the devil. Now, we know that no one is perfect. How can we avoid being a sinner, being of the devil? Each time we sin we have to admit our sin or, more precisely, say that specific sin so God can forgive us (1 John 1:9). Without repentance, God has to hold our sin against us, and we are of the devil. As soon as we repent, God forgives and covers our sin with the blood of Jesus. Instantly in Gods eyes our sin is no longer existent. It's a miracle, and it sets us free!

Repentance is a lifestyle. It is the humble condition of one who has an honest heart before God. Such a person knows his God and His mercy, forgiveness, and grace. At the same time, one who has a repentant heart can recognize the reality of the fleshly nature that is in us and the necessity to cover our sins with the blood of Jesus! There is no way to get rid of sin, except through Jesus. The goal is, of course, to develop a disciplined lifestyle that helps us stay free from sin as much as we can. With the power of the Holy Spirit we can and we should be that kind of overcomer.

## Humanism Is of the Devil

Peter was a faithful and spiritual person who could see spiritual things. Matthew 16:16–19 tells how Peter received the greatest revelation about who Jesus really was and then was given a fantastic prophetic word from Jesus. Nevertheless, Peter fell right back into his human, fleshly nature when Jesus began to tell His disciples that He must go to Jerusalem to suffer and be killed.

> Then Peter took Him aside to speak to Him privately and began to reprove and charge Him sharply, saying, God forbid, Lord! This must never happen to You! But Jesus turned away from Peter and said to him, Get behind Me, Satan! You are in My way [an offense and a hindrance

and a snare to Me]; for you are minding what partakes not of the nature and quality of God, but of men.

—Matthew 16:22–23, amp

How rude of Jesus to rebuke someone who had only good intensions! Wasn't it obvious that Peter was concerned about Jesus' well-being? More than Peter's good intentions and concern for Jesus, this scripture shows that Peter did not want anything to cause him to lose Jesus. Peter was driven by fear as he tried to stop Jesus from God's plan and calling for Him. Fear that is covered with humanism kills God's plan and calling for us.

Whether it is a person, a religion, or a spirit that tries to get in the way of salvation according to Jesus, it is of the devil. Is Islam of the devil? Is it the way to the truth and to happiness? Is it the way to eternal life? Can you be forgiven by Islam? Did Mohammed die for your sin? Was he crucified and resurrected? Of course, we know the answer; it is no. So what would Jesus do? Would Jesus put up a sign in His yard? Yes, He would!

Actually, Jesus did put up a sign. In John 14:6 Jesus said, "I am the way and the truth and the life." He said there is no other way to salvation, to the Father, to heaven except through Him. This was a very bold statement. Many people who wrote us positive e-mails said that the sign we put up was a very bold statement. Yes, Jesus would put a sign up in His yard. He was that radical.

## Christians Are Not Influencing the World

Our message appeared in newspapers and on TV and YouTube. The YouTube response we received was a surprise to us, an eye-opener to the fact that we as Christians are not influencing the world, the society, or the government as we should. We are not influencing the school system or the business area. Our YouTube presentation declared a message every true, born-again believer should support: "There is one way to God, and that way is Jesus Christ." Most of our response came from Muslims who expressed their outrage against this and voiced their support for the Quran. However, few Christians or churches would take a stand, not even to say that they believed in the truth of the sign but not our approach.

The reason we received little response from Christians and churches is that they do not get involved. We found many, many people who believe the message of the sign but hide behind slogans like "God will do it. God is in control." The truth is, God did not build the ark. He gave instructions to Noah, but He did not build the ark. Noah and his family built it. Hebrews 6:10 says, "God is not unjust; he will not forget your work and the love you have shown him as you have helped his people and continue to help them." Although this verse promises that God will not forget our work, we as Christians have forgotten how to work!

We who are pastors and Christian leaders have been ministering to the saints. However, let us take a closer look at what we do and ask. What is ministering? It is indeed talking, sharing, encouraging, and comforting. But it also is telling the truth. The truth shall set us free, especially, telling the truth about Islam or other religions.

Mohammed said:

> The judgment day will not come before the Muslim fight the Jews. And the Muslim will kill the Jews. And then the Jews will hide behind stones or trees. And the stone and the tree will say: oh Muslim, oh servant of Allah, here is a Jew behind me, come and kill him.
> —Sahih Muslim, Book 041, Number 6985

That is the religion that Muslims serve. However, the religion we serve declares John 3:16: "God so loved the world, that he gave his only begotten Son" (kjv). Our sign, our message, is a challenge to Muslims to search for the truth that the only true God is found in Jesus Christ alone. It is a challenge to Christians to take a stand and not be ashamed of the truth that sets us free. In 1 Samuel 17:45, when David fought Goliath, he said, "I come against you in the name of the Lord." We, like David, have to remember who our God is! Yes, our sign is a call for Christians to repent and to finally stand and fight the good fight of faith!

## Jesus Confronted the People of His Day

The condition of the church can be compared with the condition of our society. Our main problem is selfishness and a huge lack of discipline. Especially in the church, these issues have manifested so strongly that if you preach on them, people become angry and leave. As we consider this, we need to look at Jesus' ministry and see how He confronted people and called them to repentance.

Even before Jesus started preaching, John the Baptist spoke to the people and called them to repentance (Matt. 3). The message of repentance includes telling people about their sins, and John the Baptist confronted the Pharisees and Sadducees, the religious leaders of that time, with their false and lying lifestyle in a very direct way. He preached the truth about what God wants and how they did not live up to it. Matthew 14 tells how John the Baptist was arrested because he confronted the governor about his immorality. Later he was beheaded.

In Matthew 6 Jesus warned against attitudes we should not have. He told us what was important to pursue and what was useless or sinful. For example, He referred to the Pharisees when He said in verse five: "And when you pray, do not be like the hypocrites, for they love to pray standing in the synagogues and on the street corners to be seen by men." The Pharisees were mad at Jesus throughout His earthly ministry. They were thinking only about how to kill Him because He told the truth about them!

After the prayer Jesus taught us, He talked about forgiveness:

> For if you forgive men when they sin against you, your heavenly Father will also forgive you. But if you do not forgive men their sins, your Father will not forgive your sins.
> —Matthew 6:14–15

The truth about this verse is that if people in general have problems forgiving others, there is a big chance that they might have lost their salvation. We are saved not because we believe in God but because we have repented and God has forgiven us. The devil himself believes in God, and he is trembling with fear (James 2:19). We all know that the devil will not be in heaven. Without repentance there is no salvation.

If you read the Gospels carefully, you will see that Jesus was very challenging and radical in His ministry to people. Yes, He healed many people, but He always confronted and corrected them as well. In John 5:14, He told the invalid He had healed, "See, you are well again. Stop sinning or something worse may happen to you." And to the women caught in adultery He said:

> "Woman, where are they? Has no one condemned you?" "No one, sir," she said. "Then neither do I condemn you," Jesus declared. "Go now and leave your life of sin."
> —John 8:10–11

Jesus had the right to condemn the woman, and He didn't. However, He did challenge her to change. Jesus did not sweet-talk her, telling her how much God loves her and sympathizing with her because she had been through so much rejection from wicked people. No, He simply forgave her sin and told her to change.

And, Jesus was very direct in His teaching about our relationships with one another.

> If your brother wrongs you, go and show him his fault, between you and him privately. If he listens to you, you have won back your brother. But if he does not listen, take along with you one or two others, so that every

> word may be confirmed and upheld by the testimony of two or three witnesses. If he pays no attention to them [refusing to listen and obey], tell it to the church; and if he refuses to listen even to the church, let him be to you as a pagan and a tax collector.
> —Matthew 18:15–17, amp

The response of people to Jesus is no different today than it was when He walked the earth. Wherever there is action, you will always find multitudes. However, as soon as things become challenging and require some commitment, the multitudes disappear instantly—usually not calmly but with loads of accusations. This is what happened in John 6:25–66. After Jesus fed the five thousand earlier in the chapter, the crowd followed Him to the other side of the Sea of Galilee. They were people like you and me, following Jesus to receive a blessing. That is fine, but we must not follow Jesus only for the purpose of getting something.

Jesus confronted the crowd with the fact that they had come looking for Him because He had fed them. He challenged them to seek Him not "for food that spoils, but for food that endures to eternal life" (John 6:27). After Jesus continued with strong teaching about His identity as the Bread of Life (John 6:35), the crowd and even many of His disciples turned away from following Him. Yet, this did not stop Jesus from telling the truth, and it should not stop us either. And I wonder, will we, like the disciples who stopped following Jesus long ago, also leave Jesus when He confronts us with truth?

When Jesus spoke to Nicodemus, a Pharisee who came to talk to Him one night, He was not afraid to speak truth very directly to him:

> Jesus said, "You're a respected teacher of Israel and you don't know these basics? Listen carefully. I'm speaking sober truth to you. I speak only of what I know by experience; I give witness only to what I have seen with my own eyes. There is nothing secondhand here, no hearsay. Yet instead of facing the evidence and accepting it, you procrastinate with questions. If I tell you things that are plain as the hand before your face and you don't believe me, what use is there in telling you of things you can't see, the things of God?"
> —John 3:10–12, the message

And when He addressed a group of Pharisees, Jesus was equally as strong.

> "If God were your father," said Jesus, "you would love me, for I came from God and arrived here. I didn't come on my own. He sent me. Why can't you understand one word I say? Here's why: You can't handle it. You're from your father, the Devil, and all you want to do is please him.

He was a killer from the very start. He couldn't stand the truth because there wasn't a shred of truth in him. When the Liar speaks, he makes it up out of his lying nature and fills the world with lies. I arrive on the scene, tell you the plain truth, and you refuse to have a thing to do with me. Can any one of you convict me of a single misleading word, a single sinful act? But if I'm telling the truth, why don't you believe me? Anyone on God's side listens to God's words. This is why you're not listening—because you're not on God's side."

—John 8:42–47, the message

As we read the Scriptures, we receive ample proof that we are in good company when we stand up and speak the truth. It is very interesting to see how Jesus used to teach and correct His twelve disciples. Especially after His resurrection, He was very strict and firm with them. And when we read the letters the apostles wrote, we understand that their entire lives gave proof of being radical and challenging, always involved in work for the kingdom of God.

The Book of James, which was written by James the brother of Jesus, speaks very directly to us as Christians about having genuine faith that will express itself in our actions. It causes us to consider if we will take a stand for truth in our response to Islam with these words:

Dear friends, do you think you'll get anywhere in this if you learn all the right words but never do anything? Does merely talking about faith indicate that a person really has it? For instance, you come upon an old friend dressed in rags and half-starved and say, "Good morning, friend! Be clothed in Christ! Be filled with the Holy Spirit!" and walk off without providing so much as a coat or a cup of soup—where does that get you? Isn't it obvious that God-talk without God-acts is outrageous nonsense?

I can already hear one of you agreeing by saying, "Sounds good. You take care of the faith department, I'll handle the works department." Not so fast. You can no more show me your works apart from your faith than I can show you my faith apart from my works. Faith and works, works and faith, fit together hand in glove. Do I hear you professing to believe in the one and only God, but then observe you complacently sitting back as if you had done something wonderful? That's just great. Demons do that, but what good does it do them? Use your heads! Do you suppose for a minute that you can cut faith and works in two and not end up with a corpse on your hands?

—James 2:14–20, the message

We have seen how Jesus confronted the people of His day and called them to repentance, and there can be no doubt that He would do the same if He were physically here today. So I repeat the question I asked at the beginning of this chapter: What would Jesus say about Islam?

# Part II
# Who Is the Head of Today's Church?

# The CHURCH MUST TAKE ACTION

PEOPLE ARE BEGINNING TO RECOGNIZE Islam as an evil, oppressive, violent religion that has become a global threat. We have seen terrible things happen through terrorist attacks here in the United States and in many places all over the world. Many books have been written by people who have done intense research on all the facts that prove the evil of Islam and the danger behind it. The Internet is overflowing with evidence that women have been abused, Christians have been killed, and churches have been burned by radical Muslims.

So what do we do with this knowledge and understanding that we have become vulnerable to the evil of Islam? We as the church must take action against Islam by standing for truth, as God has called us to do. We have to make a difference in any way and with anything possible. We must actively express our opinion about the danger of Islam in spite of the resistance we receive from Christians, the community, the government, and simply from people who follow the crowd.

In Revelation 3:9 Jesus spoke to the church in Philadelphia and said:

> Behold, I will cause those of the synagogue of Satan, who say that they are Jews and are not, but lie—I will make them come and bow down at your feet, and make them know that I have loved you. (NAS)

This very heavy scripture gives a warning to the synagogue of Satan. Why? Did the people in the synagogue do great, horrible sins? No, they were pretending to be Jews when they really were not. They were lying about something very important to God!

How many of our Christian churches pretend to be a part of the body of Christ? What about the church you attend? What about the church down the street and around the corner? God still calls some churches a church of Satan. How many churches say they are representing Jesus but really are churches of Satan because they do not preach the gospel?

What about you? Do you wave the Christian flag? Do you say, "Yes, I

# The Church Must Take Action

believe in God. I am a Christian?" Are you a Christian, or are you a liar? Notice what the Bible says about liars:

> We know that the law is good if one uses it properly. We also know that law is made not for the righteous but for lawbreakers and rebels, the ungodly and sinful, the unholy and irreligious; for those who kill their fathers or mothers, for murderers, for adulterers and perverts, for slave traders and *liars* and perjurers—and for whatever else is contrary to the sound doctrine that conforms to the glorious gospel of the blessed God, which he entrusted to me.
>
> —1 Timothy 1:8, emphasis added

Are you a Christian who does not stand up and witness of His truth? Are you a Christian who does not take the opportunities that God has given you? God calls you to repent and stand up for the truth! We must stand up before it is too late. If we do not, sooner or later it will be too late.

We, the United States of America, as well as we, the church, have to face a challenge and this is no secret. Islam is out there waiting for its chance to claim our nation. And they are not to blame. We are! We in the church are to blame because we knew better than to preach a comfortable life of health, happiness, and prosperity. We knew that we should preach the truth of repentance so God could bless this nation again. The United States of America was founded by bold and brave men who had faith in the God of the Bible. Those days when God was with this nation are gone, but it is not too late to repent and come back to the Lord our God!

I have observed that the church has almost completely lost its vision and purpose. It has strayed away from the vision of being the overcoming church, the church that is ruling and reigning, influencing the society and changing it for good. That is what apostolic ministry is about. However, people today like the prophetic, because it gives them dreams and visions and tells them what is going to happen. It talks about how to survive what is coming, and it does not put a demand on them.

In the church today, we talk about having a better life and stress management and debt relief. These are topics we should talk about in the church, but they are not the call and vision of the church. Rather, the church is called to action. It is about overcoming, and its purpose is not acceptance but change!

God has given us a way to overcome the problems in our nation in this End Time. First Chronicles 12:32 tells the men of Issachar were among those who came to David at Hebron to help turn Saul's kingdom over to him. These men of Issachar are described in that verse as those "who understood the times and knew what Israel should do." They recognized that it was a new time, the time for a new leader. Today we have to recognize the times, not to conform to them but to change them. The Bible says that God has given us the answer, but not in our church programs or in making our church members friendly so people will be attracted. Rather, the answer is preaching and teaching about facing the challenges of our times.

We must return to discipline and order in the church if we are to fulfill our call and destiny as the body of Christ. What we have now is chaos. Everybody is doing what they want to do, as the Bible says of Israel in Deuteronomy 12:8. In every aspect of society and also in the church there must be order. We must submit to the order and vision God has given His church. If God has brought you to a particular church, you must pick up the vision God has given to the leadership He has established in that church. This is necessary if we are to become the overcoming church the Bible talks about, a church that makes a difference.

## Rebellion Against the Truth

*Freedom!* For us as Americans this is a huge word! It speaks of our right and our privilege, and it is what this nation was founded upon: religious freedom, individual freedom, freedom of speech. The Bible talks about freedom. It talks about our freedom to choose right or wrong, blessing or curse, life or death, heaven or hell. We have the freedom to choose the consequences that follow our decision. If we do not accept Jesus Christ as the Son of God and Savior, when we die we will go to hell. If we chose to believe Jesus is the Son of God and the only way to God and salvation, we will go to heaven. If we chose not to obey God's Word and His commandments, we will be cursed. If we obey God, we will be blessed. If we fail to obey, there is always God's mercy and grace to forgive our sins and failure, if we repent. With this freedom comes a responsibility not to misuse this great gift. We cannot take lightly the sacrifice of Jesus Christ, who died for us and our sins on the cross. Only because of His sacrifice do we have this freedom. We must honor it with our lives as we are obedient to God's Word. This freedom should never be used as an opportunity for the flesh or as an opportunity to rebel!

Rebellion is a great problem in our nation and a great global problem in general. Rebellion is very deceiving, and it somehow gives us a superior feeling, one of being right. People like to rebel against authority. Yet, without authority we have no order, which is necessary to make things function in all areas of life.

We have order in nature. If we look at the animals, we can see that they all follow a structure. Many animals that travel in groups have a pack leader, and all the animals in that group follow that leader. And, we must have order in society—the family, the school system, our places of employment. We rely on leadership that holds authority to provide for the function of order in society. The only place we do not have order is in the church.

America has a large number of churches, but we as Christians are not making the impact we should be making because we have no real authority and order in the church. Rather, we have people who speak and people who listen as long as they like the message. As soon as we preach something different than what people want to hear, they start to rebel. They make accusations. Americans have created a lifestyle around what they want to believe, and as soon as the message does not fit that lifestyle, people leave.

Generally speaking, we don't have the church of the New Testament anymore. The pastors of some churches are no longer preaching the Bible. Instead of preaching what God is saying, they preach what they know the people want to hear. They want the people to stay in that church and continue to give their finances. No matter how spiritual you are, you still need money to operate. We have become a friendly church, a people-orientated church.

The Bible, however, shows that the New Testament church was a different kind of church, a God-orientated church. It was not the nice church on the corner, but it was hated and persecuted. The New Testament church was hated because it preached the truth—just as John the Baptist, who preached a message of repentance and change, and Jesus, our Savior, who was God Himself, were hated.

Today the church is not hated, because we are not doing anything. We have conformed to society like a business or the school system so that people will like us and we will be accepted. When we preach the message the New Testament church preached, people rebel! And through all my years in the ministry I have never seen God bless a rebellious person or group. Even if they think they had a right to continue with their actions—even if they were right in some aspects—God did not bless their rebellion! There is no blessing upon that act.

What must be the message today in America? Of course, we are to preach the aspect of God loving and blessing us, but that is only a part of the message. He also wants us to preach about repentance, sacrifice, and making a difference in our society. People need to be told what the Bible says. The Bible is clear that we must speak the truth in love! I have found that if you do that, people do not like it. They do not like the truth. Yet, we who are spiritual leaders must stand up. We cannot be buddies with Islam. We must stand up and call the nation to repentance. This is our job, our responsibility. This is the major thing God has told us to do.

## A Weak Prophetic Ministry

The church is no longer God-centered. It has become self-centered or, in other words, people-centered. The church tells people what they want to hear, because the pastors are afraid that the people will leave their congregations and go to a different church. However, we must exercise the fivefold-ministry taught in Ephesians 4:11–16 and pass on to the saints what God is telling us to do. The prophetic ministry has become books, dreams, visions, what is going to happen; it has been reduced to merely giving encouraging words. This may be a part of the prophetic ministry, but if we look at the Bible, we see more than this.

What did the prophets in the Bible do in their time? Jonah called a whole nation to repentance. Nathan the prophet told David a tale that showed him his sin and moved him to repent. Consider Samuel and John the Baptist. They called the people to repentance! That is the job of the prophetic ministry. We have to call this nation, this people, back to God and to repentance.

Even as the New Testament was being written, its writers believed that they were living in the End Times. If they were living in the End Times then, we certainly are now. God needs us to become men and women of God, people who have their priorities straight. If the church is the body of Christ, living as men and women of God should be our first priority, and calling people to repentance must be ahead of everything else. Does the body of Jesus Christ have these priorities today? Where is the local church and its vision?

In 2 Timothy 3:2 the Bible clearly says that in the End Times people will become:

- Lovers of self. We do what we want to do instead of doing what we should do. Although this is what society and the church of today teaches us, we should instead do what the Bible says God wants us to do. We must be like Nehemiah, who obeyed God and built the wall to bring protection to Jerusalem.

- Lovers of money, boastful, proud, abusive, disobedient to parents.

- Very rebellious. As we showed in the section above, we have a very rebellious nation, and many in our country are even proud of it. Also, the church of today has become very rebellious. The Bible says that in the End Times this rebellion will grow, and we see this in society and in the church.
- Ungrateful. We have become ungrateful! Through all my years in ministry I have found that people who are ungrateful lose everything they have. For example, if a husband or a wife becomes ungrateful, the marriage will not work. The husband and wife may lose their marriage and end up with a situation that is worse than what they thought they had. If a nation or a church becomes ungrateful for its leaders, it will lose them and usually get new leaders who are worse than the former leaders.
- Unholy. The church of today has become unholy, and our people are no different than those in the world. We in the church have the same divorce rate as the world. We have a church where people, especially the young people, dress, act, sleep around, and are involved in pornography, just like the world.

We have a need for real apostolic and prophetic ministry to call the church back to holiness and gratefulness, to the life that God wants us to live. Ministers of the gospel must call the nation and the church to repentance. That is what the prophetic ministry failed to do in the past and now must do.

## Ineffective Prayer

Prayer is something that nearly everyone believes in, in some form, and probably most everyone has prayed at one time in his or her life. Prayer has been proven effective, and it is indeed a very powerful force. It has been proven scientifically that people who believe in God and people who pray and have a positive attitude are likely to recover from sickness faster than people who do not believe in God or maintain a positive attitude.

However, not every prayer is effective. When it comes to prayer, one ingredient is very necessary in order to make it effective: action! When some tragedy happens, Christians usually send out newsletters and e-mails and ask others to pray. While this is the right thing to do, Christians have a tendency to use prayer as an excuse not to do anything. Yes, we must pray, but we must also do something.

In America a strong movement to legalize abortion has resulted in the killing of millions of boys and girls. And now we are seeing a similar movement to legalize same-sex marriage nationwide. We must pray against these evil works of the devil, but prayer alone will not do the job. We must also hit the streets and demonstrate. We must exercise our First Amendment right to freedom of speech and combine it with powerful prayer. We must mobilize people, Christians!

How did we win our freedom at the birth of our nation? I am sure that many people were praying when our founding fathers were fighting for our independence. However, it was not won by prayer alone. We had to demonstrate and go to war and fight for this freedom. At that particular time, war was the answer, and if we want this freedom to remain, war might be the answer now as well. After the terror attack from 9/11 we went to war. If there is an enemy who is not willing to reason, there is only one thing to do; you have to speak the language they will understand. That language is power, and sometimes this power must be demonstrated in war!

We as Christians we must do something besides pray. We must go on the streets and demonstrate; we must go to the media—the TV and newspapers—and speak up against abortion and same-sex marriage. We have to stand up and speak against Islam! Why was the civil rights movement successful? It was successful not because it was the correct thing to do but because people were committed to it and showed it by their actions! It was successful because those people were mobilized to get out on the streets and demonstrate for their rights.

Why should the church be any different? We as Christians are called to make an impact on society, to change it. We are here to stand up for what is right. We as Christian leaders, especially those who lead large churches, must do what the leaders of the civil rights movement did! We must mobilize the church. We must come together on Sunday to pray, but we must also come together from Monday to Saturday and mobilize the people to march against the evil we are facing in our nation. We cannot hide behind prayer and e-mailed prayer requests. We must put action behind our prayers and stand up for what is right.

# The APOSTOLIC CHURCH

THE CHURCH IS SICKLY AND weak. It has fallen away from the Word of God, and it has lost its power to rule and reign over sin! The body of Christ suffers under the curse of selfishness. Religiousness and humanism are king instead of Jesus. Oh, Jesus is King, of course, sitting in heaven to the right of His Father. But He is basically cut off from His body, the church, which is running around headless, not following the instructions He gave in the Great Commission.

> Therefore go and make disciples of all nations, baptizing them in the name of the Father and of the Son and of the Holy Spirit, and teaching them to obey everything I have commanded you. And surely I am with you always, to the very end of the age.
> —MATTHEW 28:19–20

In Matthew 24 Jesus talked about the signs of the End Times. It would be worth writing a book only about this, and certainly many already have. Messages and preaching about the End Times often talk a lot about how we can survive all kinds of disasters and protect ourselves, but I never hear anything about how to change it. In the Old Testament God sent prophets to people or nations many times, and if the people repented, His prophecy would not be fulfilled. God has placed the apostolic church in the world to encourage that change today.

If this is true—and it is—we must discover what the apostolic church is. What are its characteristics, and how can it change the world? To help us answer these questions, we must first become acquainted with the term *fivefold ministry*, as it is taught in Ephesians 4:11–16:

> It was he who gave some to be apostles, some to be prophets, some to be evangelists, and some to be pastors and teachers, to prepare God's people for works of service, so that the body of Christ may be built up until we all reach unity in the faith and in the knowledge of the Son of God and become mature, attaining to the whole measure of the fullness of Christ. Then we will no longer be infants, tossed back and forth by the waves,

and blown here and there by every wind of teaching and by the cunning and craftiness of men in their deceitful scheming. Instead, speaking the truth in love, we will in all things grow up into him who is the Head, that is, Christ. From him the whole body, joined and held together by every supporting ligament, grows and builds itself up in love, as each part does its work.

*Fivefold ministry* refers to the ministry of God through five different ministry gifts He has given to His church: apostles, prophets, evangelists, pastors, and teachers. The fivefold ministry has been given "to prepare God's people for works of service." The nature of apostolic ministry is to build a strong and stable foundation through training, correction, and discipline, while the nature of prophetic ministry is to call people and nations to repentance. This is different from the call of churches led by pastors, who preach salvation and lead people to Jesus Christ in evangelistic ministry. Performing healing miracles in services, traveling, preaching on God's blessings and promises for us, and giving prophetic words adds the prophetic gift to it. Teaching on how to receive the blessings of God and make them work in our lives gives proof that the teaching ministry is present.

The church is not about entertainment. It is about perfecting and equipping the saints, not only for a better life but also to do the work. How can we perfect the saints unless the saints do what those operating in the fivefold ministry say? It is very important that the saints be equipped so that they can do the work. This is completely the opposite of what we have in church today. The church of today has a pastor who has been appointed or voted in, and the congregation expects him to do the work of the ministry.

The Bible teaches it is the pastor's job, together with those operating in the fivefold ministry, to teach the saints, train them, and get them involved in the actual work of the ministry. The saints need to go out to serve, help, pray, and evangelize people. The church is not called to come and sit. It is called to come, learn, go, and do! We have lost this aspect of the church, and without it, we will never become an overcoming church. We will continue to entertain people and slowly become more and more like the world. We have to return to the things that make a difference.

## Characteristics of an Apostolic Church

### Able to make disciples and train people, churches, and nations

This is the main characteristic of an apostolic church. We do this by obeying the instruction the apostle Paul gave us in 2 Timothy 4:2–4:

> Preach the Word; be prepared in season and out of season; correct, rebuke and encourage—with great patience and careful instruction. For the time will come when men will not put up with sound doctrine. Instead, to suit their own desires, they will gather around them a great number of teachers to say what their itching ears want to hear. They will turn their ears away from the truth and turn aside to myths.

When we are under the apostolic anointing, we can help others make a change so that many do not have to turn away from the truth! However, it will not be easy. Christians accuse and betray one another more than ever. I have experienced this myself. How is it that you can build up God's work over twenty years, and the people who spent all those years with you—dear friends and family—are able to destroy it in less than twenty days because they were being misled by betrayal and hate? There are false prophets in the church of today, and their teachings mislead the body of Christ. There is no more law and order, respect and discipline in the church. There is only one law, which allows people to do anything they want: "God loves me, God blesses me, God is love, and I will receive all promises."

> At that time many will turn away from the faith and will betray and hate each other, and many false prophets will appear and deceive many people. Because of the increase of wickedness, the love of most will grow cold, but he who stands firm to the end will be saved.
> —Matthew 24:10–13

**Fearless**

Fear is a dangerous tool that the devil successfully uses to control and dominate. The devil may, through a person, use fear to control another person or to cause him or her to hide. Fear isolates a person, and it is pure pride. Fear does not trust God but tries to save itself. Fear is not always an imagined emotion, but it can build up like that. Whether fear is real or not, the results are destructive.

Fear and control are the main components in Islam. Fear is not from God, and it is useless. Jesus gave us the Holy Spirit so we can overcome fear and be fearless!

The apostolic church trains and challenges people to overcome fear in every aspect of life. It is not afraid to step out and take a stand for truth. The apostolic church is not afraid of the consequences of this boldness, though the result may be rejection, isolation, accusation, or death. Nothing can stop the apostolic church from trying to fulfill the call and vision to build God's kingdom. No matter how many defeats it faces, no sacrifice is too hard and no effort too much. For the true apostolic church there is nothing more important than the kingdom of God. Matthew 6:33 tells us to seek first the kingdom of God, and first means first—before family, work, or hobbies.

**Confrontational in its desire for change**

Confrontation is something the apostolic church does automatically, without thinking or often even without noticing. It is natural. The apostolic ministry has very few grey zones. When the apostolic ministry appears, there is always a spiritual battle with spiritual strongholds and principalities who have been ruling the Earth since they were thrown out of heaven. The spiritual, violent force of the apostolic ministry demands that the devil give back what he has stolen. These battles are getting hotter, as we are living in the End Times!

The apostolic church is not satisfied unless there is a change in the lives of people, in the church, in society, or even in the nation. Because it is fearless, it is strong, straight, and confrontational on both a spiritual and natural level. Usually people don't like that, and it is very uncomfortable for them. Although this is understandable, it is from God; it is in the Bible. In an effort not to submit to this, people accuse true apostolic ministry of exercising wrongful control. I faced this and have suffered intensely from it in my thirty years of apostolic ministry experience. I have been compared to Hitler or even to Islam. Christians told me right to my face that they would rather live under Islam and Sharia law than under my leadership.

**Active in the fivefold ministry**

The fivefold ministry is completely present in an apostolic church. This means that a church has an apostle, prophet, evangelist, pastor, and teacher in the church every day, not merely as guest speakers. The Bible is very clear about the fact that there is work to do; the fivefold ministry should train, equip, and teach the people to do the work of the ministry. They need to teach them how to serve. This way we all will grow to maturity in Christ!

Without the fivefold ministry, we have no maturity. We can clearly see this lack in the churches today! Although we have prophets, evangelists, pastors, and teachers, the people are behaving like babies. As soon as a message other than "God loves you" is preached, people get mad and leave. Everybody comes to the service on Sundays to receive but not to serve and give and sacrifice! Babies only receive, but mature adults give. The church today is made of big babies who are receiving.

What we call the apostolic ministry today is nothing different than the fivefold ministry gifts mixed together. Real apostolic ministry brings work, discipline, endurance, and submission back into the church.

There is a lot of work to do, considering the fact that Islam wants to take over. We need to reach out and preach the truth outside of the church. The apostolic ministry needs to challenge the church to go out and evangelize to reach not only the Muslims the other groups as well!

**Unity and submission**

Without the true apostolic ministry there is no true unity, a biblical unity that is based on the truth and on submission to the truth independent of personal opinion. The condition of the body of Christ today is that of a huge baby without a head trying to walk like an adult. This headless thing is going nowhere, because it can't see. It will not accomplish anything, but it is there to produce a lot of confusion and chaos. It gets hurt all the time and cries for help or prays, "God is in control." To people in the spiritual world of darkness it is like a sitcom. They look at their watches and say, "Oh, it's Sunday morning. There's our favorite show: the headless church! That is so funny! Come on, let's watch it and have a blast!"

God gave His commands to us in His Word and told us exactly what to do. Jesus did His part and sits next to His Father, waiting until His body decides to get connected to the Head. The Holy Spirit is waiting for the Christians to repent and invite Him to strengthen them for the work that needs to be done. God has done all He can do. Now it is up to us, the teachers and pastors, evangelists and prophets to make the fivefold ministry complete by submitting to the apostolic ministry and starting the real work! Ephesians 4:11 says:

> It was he who gave some to be apostles, some to be prophets, some to be evangelists, and some to be pastors and teachers.

The apostolic ministry is mentioned first, the prophets second, and so on. The apostolic and the prophetic must go together.

> Consequently, you are no longer foreigners and aliens, but fellow citizens with God's people and members of God's household, built on the foundation of the apostles and prophets, with Christ Jesus himself as the chief cornerstone. In him the whole building is joined together and rises to become a holy temple in the Lord. And in him you too are being built together to become a dwelling in which God lives by his Spirit.
> —Ephesians 2:19–22

The prophetic ministry especially is very independent. However, to have a strong and healthy foundation, it must submit to the apostolic ministry, something that seems impossible as we consider the condition of the church today.

> When the disciples heard this [Jesus' teaching about how hard it is for a rich man to enter the kingdom of heaven], they were greatly astonished and asked, "Who then can be saved?" Jesus looked at them and said, "With man this is impossible, but with God all things are possible." Peter answered him, "We have left everything to follow you! What then will there be for us?" Jesus said to them, "I tell you the truth, at the renewal of all things, when the Son of Man sits on his glorious throne, you who have followed me will also sit on twelve thrones, judging the twelve tribes of Israel. And everyone who has left houses or brothers or sisters or father or mother or children or fields for my sake will receive a hundred times as much and will inherit eternal life. But many who are first will be last, and many who are last will be first.
> —Matthew 19:25–30

With God everything is possible. And one thing is certain, in the end when we are with God, we will be truly surprised at who will be first or last! I am convinced that we as Christians—and even more as preachers of the Word of God—need the attitude Jesus was teaching the disciples, one that declares, "Oh, Lord, have mercy. Who, then, can be saved?" (See Matthew 19:24–26.) They included themselves in this question, and they somehow received the revelation that they indeed needed the grace of God. Just following Jesus is not enough. We need the revelation of our neediness so we will humble ourselves to receive the grace that makes us able to do the work of the ministry!

> And His gifts were [varied; He Himself appointed and gave men to us] some to be apostles (special messengers), some prophets (inspired preachers and expounders), some evangelists (preachers of the Gospel, traveling missionaries), some pastors (shepherds of His flock) and teachers. His intention was the perfecting and the full equipping of the saints (His consecrated people), [that they should do] the work of ministering toward building up Christ's body (the church), [That it might develop] until we all attain oneness in the faith and in the comprehension of the [full and accurate] knowledge of the Son of God, that [we might arrive] at really mature manhood (the completeness of personality which is nothing less than the standard height of Christ's own perfection), the measure of the stature of the fullness of the Christ and the completeness found in Him.
> —Ephesians 4:11–13, amp

> So God has appointed some in the church [for His own use]: first apostles (special messengers); second prophets (inspired preachers and expounders); third teachers; then wonder-workers; then those with ability to heal the sick; helpers; administrators; [speakers in] different (unknown) tongues.
> —1 Corinthians 12:28, amp

We have to submit to the local church authority. Submission is not a weird thing, and, in fact, it is present in every aspect of our society. If you do not submit at your job, you will be fired. If you go to the university, you have to submit to their rules and regulations, to their vision and their plan. If you go to school, you have to do your homework to proceed in your studies. Submission is important. We must return to it in the church and teach the people to be willing to submit to the local church authority.

**Discipline**

We have completely lost discipline in the church. We have lost this aspect of training that we need to receive blessings of God that will remain. Even our spiritual leaders today lack discipline in their lives, and many of them are extremely overweight. Discipline makes our army work, and it makes it a strong army. You cannot find obese soldiers on the battlefield, because they cannot fight or even win. The church has always been compared to an army, and it is a lack of discipline that makes the church lose!

When you preach on discipline in the church today, people get angry and say, "You are controlling. It's all about love." Those people must read a different Bible from the one I read. The last time I read about discipline in the Bible, I found that God never separates love from discipline. In fact, God gave discipline a very high standard.

> Better a patient man than a warrior, a man who controls his temper than one who takes a city.
> —Proverbs 16:32

A person who submits to godly discipline is more pleasing in the eyes of the Lord than the one who seeks to be successful in the eyes of men. God measures us according to His standard. We don't all have the same relationship with Him. Some people—those who discipline themselves through the power of the Holy Spirit—are more pleasing to God than others.

The Bible says that in the last days the lack of discipline will become a major issue.

But mark this: There will be terrible times in the last days. People will be lovers of themselves, lovers of money, boastful, proud, abusive, disobedient to their parents, ungrateful, unholy, without love, unforgiving, slanderous, without self-control, brutal, not lovers of the good.
—2 Timothy 3:1–3

The consequences of this lack of discipline are very severe, and it leads people into destruction.

- The love of self, combined with unforgiveness, leads to hell.
- The love of money leads to death.
- The love of food leads to obesity, followed by many diseases and early death.

For the kingdom of God is not a matter of eating and drinking, but of righteousness, peace and joy in the Holy Spirit.
—Romans 14:17

Ungratefulness gives proof that people are lacking in their personal relationship with God. It cuts them off from any blessing. It takes discipline to overcome our feelings and thank God for everything, especially when things are going wrong.

God Himself is disciplined in everything He does. How could the universe function without His divine discipline? And beyond that, God gave His only Son to be brutally killed and to painfully die for our sin. God gave His everything to save us. To show respect for this sacrifice, we must discipline ourselves so He can use us to build His kingdom the way He wants it to be built. It is the least we can do.

Scripture has much to say about the contrast between discipline and the lack of discipline. First, it says discipline is love, life, and protection.

My son, do not despise the Lord's discipline and do not resent his rebuke, because the Lord disciplines those he loves, as a father the son he delights in.
—Proverbs 3:11–12

For these commands are a lamp, this teaching is a light, and the corrections of discipline are the way to life.
—Proverbs 6:23

The Lord knows the thoughts of man; he knows that they are futile. Blessed is the man you discipline, O Lord, the man you teach from your law; you grant him relief from days of trouble, till a pit is dug for the wicked.

—Psalm 94:11–13

Second, lack of discipline is death and destruction.

For a man's ways are in full view of the Lord, and he examines all his paths. The evil deeds of a wicked man ensnare him; the cords of his sin hold him fast. He will die for lack of discipline, led astray by his own great folly.

—Proverbs 5:21–23

Stern discipline awaits him who leaves the path; he who hates correction will die.

—Proverbs 15:10

Whoever loves discipline loves knowledge, but he who hates correction is stupid.

—Proverbs 12:1

## Being an Apostolic Church Is Not Optional

Western Christianity is a joke, and it is no wonder the world is mocking and laughing at it. We have made our own Bible. We have taken verses that express things like, "God loves me; He blesses me," and have ignored verses that tell us to submit or work or obey. Whenever you correct modern Christians, they accuse you of judging them or they say, "Where there is love, there is God!" And, when the definition of *love* is based on feelings and humanism, everything—including adultery and homosexuality—fits in just fine.

While it is true that God loves everyone unconditionally, we cannot live like the world and still be saved. No way! That is a lie of the devil, and it is wrong! However, if the apostolic ministry would be present in our churches, our churches would be completely different than what we have today. As I have mentioned several times in this book, the church of today has fallen away from the radical message of the gospel, which declares that Jesus Christ is the only way to salvation. We have a lot of teaching about the apostolic ministry and very good teachings and revelations, but the practical side of the apostolic church does not exist!

Today everything goes through the Internet. We have apostolic networks where people can sign up to be part of an apostolic ministry without any submission. Very good men of God called apostles travel a lot and teach about the apostolic, having conferences and great services with supernatural healings and miracles. However, this is not the characteristic of apostolic ministry. Jesus said that all these signs follow those who believe, and not every believer is an apostle!

> And He said to them, Go into all the world and preach and publish openly the good news (the Gospel) to every creature [of the whole human race]. He who believes [who adheres to and trusts in and relies on the Gospel and Him Whom it sets forth] and is baptized will be saved [from the penalty of eternal death]; but he who does not believe [who does not adhere to and trust in and rely on the Gospel and Him Whom it sets forth] will be condemned. And these attesting signs will accompany those who believe: in My name they will drive out demons; they will speak in new languages; They will pick up serpents; and [even] if they drink anything deadly, it will not hurt them; they will lay their hands on the sick, and they will get well.
>
> MARK 16:15–18, AMP

God is calling the church to fulfill the apostolic calling He has given it. If we fail to respond in obedience to this calling, the church will only continue along the same cycle it has followed through the generations: we do nothing, and nothing happens. Once in a while God supernaturally pours out His Holy Spirit, and a bunch of people get saved and healed. However, in the end it has no impact on our society. The only way to impact our society is to receive the fivefold ministry God makes available to us so that we as the church will be mobilized to do the work of the ministry in our world.

# The OVERCOMING CHURCH

WHILE ISLAM IS GROWING AND daily establishing plans and strategies to take over the world, the church, lazily sitting in an armchair, is waiting to be entertained. Christians, especially young ones, think there is nothing they can do against the evil of Islam. They are deeply convinced that they cannot make a difference, so they just go on with their lives as usual. They think that by closing their eyes and waiting things out, all the problems will be solved. They seem to believe that when Jesus comes back everything will be fine.

This reminds me of how the Israelites didn't do anything but live in fear of the giant Goliath for forty days until David opposed him and killed him (1 Sam. 17). However, it does not reflect what God wants, and all Christians who think this way would be desperately disturbed if Jesus would come back right now! The Bible is very, very clear about the condition of the church that God not only wants but needs to save unbelievers and to fulfill His plan here on Earth. He calls us to be an overcoming church and practice the truth and instructions of His Word.

## The Overcoming Church Obeys God's Commandments

> Everyone who believes that Jesus is the Christ is born of God, and everyone who loves the father loves his child as well. This is how we know that we love the children of God: by loving God and carrying out his commands. This is love for God: to obey his commands. And his commands are not burdensome, for everyone born of God overcomes the world. This is the victory that has overcome the world, even our faith. Who is it that overcomes the world? Only he who believes that Jesus is the Son of God.
>
> —1 JOHN 5:1–5

God wants the church to overcome the world. To do so, we must believe that Jesus is the Son of God. If we do this, we will obey God's commandments. If we do not obey God's commands, we should consider if we are born again. We might call ourselves Christians, but are we really? If parents and pastors do not correct their teenagers when they drink, take drugs, and commit sexual sin, those kids may still go to church. However, without repentance they will go to hell when they die!

Carrying the title *Christian* does not make us world overcomers. The church has not yet overcome the world. In fact, many Christian young people almost completely live like the world does because they are influenced by TV, media, money, music, Internet, fashion, and everything else that belongs to the world. We kill thousands of unborn children every day. We are about to lose the God-given frame for a family because many support sinful lifestyles. Churches already have homosexual ministers.

To overcome the world, which is God's call for the church, we must obey His commandments. This we can do, and we have a desire to do it—if we are from God, born again, believing in Jesus Christ, the Son of God!

### The Overcoming Church Does Not Tolerate Sin

> How great is the love the Father has lavished on us, that we should be called children of God! And that is what we are! The reason the world does not know us is that it did not know him. Dear friends, now we are children of God, and what we will be has not yet been made known. But we know that when he appears, we shall be like him, for we shall see him as he is. Everyone who has this hope in him purifies himself, just as he is pure. Everyone who sins breaks the law; in fact, sin is lawlessness. But you know that he appeared so that he might take away our sins. And in him is no sin. No one who lives in him keeps on sinning. No one who continues to sin has either seen him or known him. Dear children, do not let anyone lead you astray. He who does what is right is righteous, just as he is righteous. He who does what is sinful is of the devil, because the devil has been sinning from the beginning. The reason the Son of God appeared was to destroy the devil's work. No one who is born of God will continue to sin, because God's seed remains in him; he cannot go on sinning, because he has been born of God. This is how we know who the children of God are and who the children of the devil are: Anyone who does not do what is right is not a child of God; nor is anyone who does not love his brother.
>
> —1 John 3:1–10

The Bible cannot be clearer concerning sin. You cannot be a Christian and continue to have a sinful lifestyle. If you try to talk to some Christians about this issue, they accuse you of judging them. They use the Bible to cover up their sinful lifestyle. Parents with ungodly children, even pastors, argue, "We are family; we do not point out the weaknesses." The Bible does not point out weaknesses; it exposes sin so we can repent, bring it to the cross, and receive forgiveness through the blood of Jesus. Then we have to change our life. After Jesus told the woman caught in adultery that He did not condemn her, He said, "Go now and leave your life of sin" (John 8:11).

Sin is not merely a weakness. It is a serious thing, the breaking of God's law, and it caused Jesus to die on the cross. God cannot allow sin in His presence. There is no sin in heaven, and it never will be there. Professing Christians who continue to live a sinful lifestyle are not saved and will go to hell if they do not repent. The Bible says that faith comes from hearing the message (Rom. 10:17). It is the responsibility of a pastor to preach so people turn away from sin. If a pastor is not living up to his responsibility, he leads God's children astray. Pastors today don't preach this; they teach on healing and prosperity instead. God wants to make us an overcoming church by changing our lives through the preaching of His Word.

> But if anyone causes one of these little ones who believe in me to sin, it would be better for him to have a large millstone hung around his neck and to be drowned in the depths of the sea. Woe to the world because of the things that cause people to sin! Such things must come, but woe to the man through whom they come!
> —Matthew 18:6–7

The church in general quit preaching against sin, because people don't like it. Preaching against sin has become touchy and is considered as "judging or controlling. Our church members go to the streets of Gainesville, Florida, the 11th gayest city in the US,[1] evangelizing several times per week. We preach against homosexuality, against other "possible-ways" to God than Jesus; for example, Islam. The response from Christians and others is terrifying. It shows how far away Christians have come from the Bible. They tell us, and believe it, that there are other ways to God than Jesus. Jesus Himself said in John 14:6 that He is the only way! Many times those Christians become aggressive toward us, yelling or spitting at our people and calling them all kinds of names that I don't want to repeat. You would not believe what can come out of a Christian's mouth.

In one point Christians and non-Christians agree: they call us hate preachers. They use the argument that only God can see into people's hearts and God alone can judge, giving pastors all the room they need to step away from their responsibility to preach the entire truth. The church started making compromises to win the people long ago. I think that this development has gone too far. The church tolerates pastors like Joel Osteen, who was invited to pray for the lesbian mayor in Houston.[2]

A pastor like Joel Osteen has influence and responsibility more than any other pastor because of the size of his church. He had the chance to speak up for God, the Bible, and the truth. He had the chance to be an example for others to follow the right way. He did not take that chance, and God will hold him responsible for this. Osteen lead many people astray. In my opinion, he is not saved himself. God holds us as pastors and ministers, the leaders of God's churches, responsible. Woe to us if we do not speak the truth!

> Son of man, I've made you a watchman for the family of Israel. Whenever you hear me say something, warn them for me. If I say to the wicked, "You are going to die," and you don't sound the alarm warning them that it's a matter of life or death, they will die and it will be your fault. I'll hold you responsible. But if you warn the wicked and they keep right on sinning anyway, they'll most certainly die for their sin, but you won't die. You'll have saved your life. And if the righteous turn back from living righteously and take up with evil when I step in and put them in a hard place, they'll die. If you haven't warned them, they'll die because of their sins, and none of the right things they've done will count for anything—and I'll hold you responsible. But if you warn these righteous people not to sin and they listen to you, they'll live because they took the warning—and again, you'll have saved your life.
> —Ezekiel 3:17–21, The Message

## The Overcoming Church Honors Covenant Relationships

God is a covenant God! Every word God says is followed by action, and He has confirmed the most important promises with a covenant. The church is very important to God. The relationship between God and His church, the body of His only Son, Jesus Christ, is established in a blood covenant in which He sacrificed Jesus. With this covenant God took a stand on the side of the church—whether she is good or bad, ugly or beautiful, rebellious or obedient. Indeed, He would prefer that the church be beautiful rather than ugly, and He is working to make this happen. However, the covenant is not dependent on how she looks.

Although God does not agree with many things the church is doing today, He stands loyal to His church, just as He stands loyal to His chosen nation, Israel. Loyalty comes with a covenant, or we do not have a covenant. In our covenant relationship with God, we as the church must choose biblical truth and, with loyalty to Him, obey it. Loyalty has nothing to do with agreement on how things are handled. It is standing true to our covenant with God, even when we do not agree with everything He is doing.

God compares His relationship with His church to a marriage covenant. A marriage only works when the husband and wife are loyal to one another, independent of right or wrong that the other may do. It needs love, of course love, but more than that, it needs trust and the will to make it work. The husband and wife each must know their respective parts in the marriage covenant and be loyal to it. The same goes for the church, as the apostle Paul explained.

> Wives, submit to your husbands as to the Lord. For the husband is the head of the wife as Christ is the head of the church, his body, of which he is the Savior. Now as the church submits to Christ, so also wives should submit to their husbands in everything. Husbands, love your wives, just as Christ loved the church and gave himself up for her to make her holy, cleansing her by the washing with water through the word, and to present her to himself as a radiant church, without stain or wrinkle or any other blemish, but holy and blameless. In this same way, husbands ought to love their wives as their own bodies. He who loves his wife loves himself. After all, no one ever hated his own body, but he feeds and cares for it, just as Christ does the church—for we are members of his body. "For this reason a man will leave his father and mother and be united to his wife, and the two will become one flesh." This is a profound mystery—but I am talking about Christ and the church. However, each one of you also must love his wife as he loves himself, and the wife must respect her husband.
> —Ephesians 5:22–33

Marriage is not popular anymore, and it seems that we are about to lose the structure God has provided to make living and society stable. Besides the fact that some choose homosexuality, the divorce rate is going up each year. Many young people somehow do not have a strong desire to get married anymore. And we have no submission anymore, in marriage or in the church. This is why the church is weak and cannot fulfill its destiny to overcome the world.

The church of today longs for "goose bumps love" experiences, but as soon as a challenge comes, the love goes away; the covenant is broken. Yet, loyalty and commitment come along with our covenant relationship with God. Even though the church of today does not like this, it is still the Word of God. And, it is still the way God wants His church, the overcoming church to be.

## The Overcoming Church Does Not Love the World

Do not love the world or anything in the world. If anyone loves the world, the love of the Father is not in him. For everything in the world—the cravings of sinful man, the lust of his eyes and the boasting of what he has and does—comes not from the Father but from the world. The world and its desires pass away, but the man who does the will of God lives forever.

—1 John 2:15–16

The man who does not do the will of God but follows his own desires will live forever, but not with God. He will live forever in hell, no matter how many times he proclaims, "God loves me. God is love. God loves me!" There must be a difference between the church and the world. God is searching for a remnant, for those who want to forsake what the world offers and love the Father instead.

## The Overcoming Church Tests the Spirits

Dear friends, do not believe every spirit, but test the spirits to see whether they are from God, because many false prophets have gone out into the world. This is how you can recognize the Spirit of God: Every spirit that acknowledges that Jesus Christ has come in the flesh is from God, but every spirit that does not acknowledge Jesus is not from God. This is the spirit of the antichrist, which you have heard is coming and even now is already in the world. You, dear children, are from God and have overcome them, because the one who is in you is greater than the one who is in the world. They are from the world and therefore speak from the viewpoint of the world, and the world listens to them. We are from God, and whoever knows God listens to us; but whoever is not from God does not listen to us. This is how we recognize the Spirit of truth and the spirit of falsehood.

—1 John 4:1–6

Just as the Pharisees accused Jesus of casting out demons by Beelzebub in Matthew 12:24, the lukewarm church accuses the true church of being a false prophet or being controlling. However, the true church will be radical in its obedience to Scripture, and it will make a clear difference between right and wrong, a right spirit and a wrong spirit. The Bible tells us to test the spirits, to recognize them, and then, of course, to overcome the wrong one! God is greater than the evil one who is in the world, and you are able to overcome evil if He is in you. If you never overcome anything, examine your heart; it could be that God is not in you, as you think.

## The Overcoming Church Has Sacrificial Love

> Dear friends, let us love one another, for love comes from God. Everyone who loves has been born of God and knows God. Whoever does not love does not know God, because God is love. This is how God showed his love among us: He sent his one and only Son into the world that we might live through him. This is love: not that we loved God, but that he loved us and sent his Son as an atoning sacrifice for our sins. Dear friends, since God so loved us, we also ought to love one another. No one has ever seen God; but if we love one another, God lives in us and his love is made complete in us.
>
> —1 John 4:7–12

What does the apostle John mean when he says, "God lives in us and his love is made complete in us"? Does it mean that we do not need to change? If God is living in us anyway and we are complete, why do we have to obey God's commandments and quit sinning? This is where we easily lose what God really wants from us. We don't want to change, so we ignore the part about obedience and not sinning and take only that part about God loving us. We forget that the love of God is a sacrificing love. When God is really in us, we also have an ability to love sacrificially because that is God's character. It is His heart.

## The Overcoming Church Is Repentant

> To the angel of the church in Ephesus write.... Remember the height from which you have fallen! Repent and do the things you did at first. If you do not repent, I will come to you and remove your lampstand from its place.... He who has an ear, let him hear what the Spirit says to the churches. To him who overcomes, I will give the right to eat from the tree of life, which is in the paradise of God.
>
> —Revelation 2:1, 5, 7

To the angel of the church in Pergamum write.... Nevertheless, I have a few things against you: You have people there who hold to the teaching of Balaam, who taught Balak to entice the Israelites to sin by eating food sacrificed to idols and by committing sexual immorality. Likewise you also have those who hold to the teaching of the Nicolaitans. Repent therefore! Otherwise, I will soon come to you and will fight against them with the sword of my mouth. He who has an ear, let him hear what the Spirit says to the churches. To him who overcomes, I will give some of the hidden manna. I will also give him a white stone with a new name written on it, known only to him who receives it.

—Revelation 2:12, 14–17

To the angel of the church in Thyatira write.... Nevertheless, I have this against you: You tolerate that woman Jezebel, who calls herself a prophetess. By her teaching she misleads my servants into sexual immorality and the eating of food sacrificed to idols. I have given her time to repent of her immorality, but she is unwilling. So I will cast her on a bed of suffering, and I will make those who commit adultery with her suffer intensely, unless they repent of her ways. I will strike her children dead. Then all the churches will know that I am he who searches hearts and minds, and I will repay each of you according to your deeds. Now I say to the rest of you in Thyatira, to you who do not hold to her teaching and have not learned Satan's so-called deep secrets (I will not impose any other burden on you): Only hold on to what you have until I come. To him who overcomes and does my will to the end, I will give authority over the nations—'He will rule them with an iron scepter; he will dash them to pieces like pottery'—just as I have received authority from my Father. I will also give him the morning star. He who has an ear, let him hear what the Spirit says to the churches.

—Revelation 2:18, 20–29

To the angel of the church in Sardis write: These are the words of him who holds the seven spirits of God and the seven stars. I know your deeds; you have a reputation of being alive, but you are dead. Wake up! Strengthen what remains and is about to die, for I have not found your deeds complete in the sight of my God. Remember, therefore, what you have received and heard; obey it, and repent. But if you do not wake up, I will come like a thief, and you will not know at what time I will come to you. Yet you have a few people in Sardis who have not soiled their clothes. They will walk with me, dressed in white, for they are worthy. He who overcomes will, like them, be dressed in white. I will never blot out his name from the book of life, but will acknowledge his name before my Father and his angels. He who has an ear, let him hear what the Spirit says to the churches.

—Revelation 3:1–6

To the angel of the church in Laodicea write: These are the words of the Amen, the faithful and true witness, the ruler of God's creation. I know your deeds, that you are neither cold nor hot. I wish you were either one or the other! So, because you are lukewarm—neither hot nor cold—I am about to spit you out of my mouth. You say, 'I am rich; I have acquired wealth and do not need a thing.' But you do not realize that you are wretched, pitiful, poor, blind and naked. I counsel you to buy from me gold refined in the fire, so you can become rich; and white clothes to wear, so you can cover your shameful nakedness; and salve to put on your eyes, so you can see. Those whom I love I rebuke and discipline. So be earnest, and repent. Here I am! I stand at the door and knock. If anyone hears my voice and opens the door, I will come in and eat with him, and he with me. To him who overcomes, I will give the right to sit with me on my throne, just as I overcame and sat down with my Father on his throne. He who has an ear, let him hear what the Spirit says to the churches."

—Revelation 3:14–22

## The Overcoming Church Is Persecuted

To the angel of the church in Smyrna write: These are the words of him who is the First and the Last, who died and came to life again. I know your afflictions and your poverty—yet you are rich! I know the slander of those who say they are Jews and are not, but are a synagogue of Satan. Do not be afraid of what you are about to suffer. I tell you, the devil will put some of you in prison to test you, and you will suffer persecution for ten days. Be faithful, even to the point of death, and I will give you the crown of life. He who has an ear, let him hear what the Spirit says to the churches. He who overcomes will not be hurt at all by the second death.

—Revelation 2:8–11

To the angel of the church in Philadelphia write: These are the words of him who is holy and true, who holds the key of David. What he opens no one can shut, and what he shuts no one can open. I know your deeds. See, I have placed before you an open door that no one can shut. I know that you have little strength, yet you have kept my word and have not denied my name. I will make those who are of the synagogue of Satan, who claim to be Jews though they are not, but are liars—I will make them come and fall down at your feet and acknowledge that I have loved you. Since you have kept my command to endure patiently, I will also keep you from the hour of trial that is going to come upon the whole world to test those who live on the earth. I am coming soon. Hold on to what you have, so that no one will take your crown. Him who overcomes I will make a pillar in the temple of my God. Never again will he leave it. I will write on him the name of my God and the name of the city of my God, the new Jerusalem, which is coming down out of heaven from my God; and I will also write on him my new name. He who has an ear, let him hear what the Spirit says to the churches.

—Revelation 3:7–13

## The Overcoming Church Is Victorious and Free

Revelation 12:11 tells us how we overcome the devil and, yes, the evil of Islam.

> They overcame him by the blood of the Lamb and by the word of their testimony; they did not love their lives so much as to shrink from death.
> —Revelation 12:11

We overcome by the blood of the Lamb. The prophets of Islam did not give their blood for us; rather, they are the cause of shedding blood. Also, we overcome by the word of our testimony. In other words, we have to stand up and not hide behind religious excuses such as, "What about this?" "What about that?" "You could have done that." Or, "Why did you do it that way?" We have to stand up and point people in the right direction. The Bible says that we are not to love our life, even when we are faced with death; victory and freedom are won because people are willing to put their lives on the line.

# The PERSECUTED CHURCH

WHEN WE AS THE CHURCH choose to take a stand for truth against the evil of Islam, we can expect to suffer persecution. The church has suffered persecution from the very beginning. There was never really a time when the radical church had peace in this world. In fact, Jesus told us that if we followed Him, we would be persecuted.

> If you belonged to the world, it would love you as its own. As it is, you do not belong to the world, but I have chosen you out of the world. That is why the world hates you. Remember the words I spoke to you: 'No servant is greater than his master.' If they persecuted me, they will persecute you also. If they obeyed my teaching, they will obey yours also. They will treat you this way because of my name, for they do not know the One who sent me.
>
> —John 15:19–21

In this chapter, we will see how radical Christians have suffered for their faith in Christ and their commitment to show it by their actions. They have experienced persecution throughout the centuries since Jesus rose from the dead and ascended to heaven, and they continue to suffer for His name at this present time. Persecution has come to them from a variety of sources, including the Islamic world.

### Persecution of Early Christians in Palestine*

The early Christians were considered originally a Jewish religious sect, emerged in Roman Judea in the first century AD. The Pharisees, including Paul, before he converted to Christianity, persecuted the early Christians, who preached a Messiah which did not conform to the expectations of the time. Dissention began almost immediately

---

\* This material is taken from the Wikipedia page for Persecution of Christians found at http://en.wikipedia.org/wiki/Persecution_of_Christians, accessed April 30, 2010. The text is available under the Creative Commons Attribution-ShareAlike License, http://creativecommons.org/licenses/by-sa/3.0/.

with the unorthodox teaching by Stephen at Jerusalem, and never ceased entirely while the city remained. A year after the crucifixion Stephen was stoned for his transgression, Saul heartily agreeing (who later converted and was renamed "Paul"). In A.D. 41, when Agrippa I, who already possessed the territory of Antipas and Phillip, obtained the power of the procurator in Judea, hence reforming the Kingdom of Herod, he was eager to endear himself to his Jewish subjects and continued the persecution in which James the lesser lost his life, Peter narrowly escaped and the rest of the apostles took flight. After Agrippa's death, procuratorship resumed and those leaders maintained a neutral peace, until the procurator Festus died and the high priest Annas II took advantage of the power vacuum to attack the Church and executed James the greater, then leader of Jerusalem's Christians. The New Testament says that Paul was himself imprisoned on several occasions by the Roman authorities, stoned by Pharisees and left for dead on one occasion, and was eventually taken as a prisoner to Rome. Peter and others were also imprisoned, beaten and generally harassed. The Roman killing of 3,000 Jews incited a revolt leading to the destruction of Jerusalem in A.D. 70, the end of sacrificial Judaism, and the disempowering the persecutors; the Christian community, meanwhile, having fled to safety in the already pacified region of Pella. The early persecution by the Jews is estimated to have a death toll of about 2,000. The Jewish persecutions were trivial when compared with the brutal and widespread persecution by the Romans. Of the eleven remaining apostles (Judas Iscariot having killed himself), only one—John, the son of Zebedee and Salome, the younger brother of James and the writer of the Book of Revelation—died of natural causes in exile. The other ten were reportedly martyred by various means including beheading, by sword and spear and, in the case of Peter, crucifixion upside down following the execution of his wife. The New Testament relates the Christian accounts of the Pharisee rejection of Jesus and accusations of the Pharisee responsibility for his crucifixion. The Acts of the Apostles depicts instances of early Christian persecution by the Sanhedrin, the Hebrew religious establishment of the time. This theme plays an important part in a number of Christian doctrines ranging from the release of Christians from obeying the many strictures of the Old Testament Law to the commandment to preach to all nations meaning to Gentiles as well as the Hebrew people.

## Persecution of Early Christians in the Roman Empire

There was the Persecution under Nero, 64-68 AD, the Persecution from the second century to Constantine and the Great Persecution.

The religion gradually spread out of Judea, initially establishing major bases in first Antioch, then Alexandria, and over time throughout the Roman Empire. For the first two centuries, the imperial authorities largely viewed Christianity simply as a Jewish sect rather than a distinct religion. Tacitus reports that after the Great Fire of Rome in AD 64 some in the population held Nero responsible and that to diffuse blame, he targeted and blamed the Christians. The war against the Jews during Nero's reign, which so destabilized the empire that it led to the first civil war since the days of Julius Caesar and Mark Antony, as well as Nero's suicide, plausibly provided an additional rationale for persecutions against this "Jewish" sect. Persecution of Christians would be a recurring theme in the Empire for the next two centuries. Eusebius and Lactantius document the last great persecution of the Christians under Diocletian at the beginning of the 4th century at the urging of Galerius. This was the most vicious persecution of Christians in the Empire's history. After Diocletian, however, the fact that emperors were often Christians themselves lessened whatever persecutions may have still been occurring. As the 4th century progressed, Christianity had become so widespread that it became officially tolerated, then promoted, and in 380 etablished as the Empire's official religion. By the 5th century Christianity had become the Empire's predominant religion rapidly changing the Empire's identity even as the Western provinces collapsed.

The Diocletianic Persecution (or Great Persecution) was the last and most severe persecution of Christians in the Roman empire. In 303, Emperor Diocletian and his colleagues Maximian, Galerius, and Constantius issued a series of edicts rescinding the legal rights of Christians and demanding that they comply with traditional religious practices. Later edicts targeted the clergy and demanded universal sacrifice, ordering all inhabitants to sacrifice to the gods. The persecution varied in intensity across the empire—weakest in Gaul and Britain, where only the first edict was applied, and strongest in the Eastern provinces. Persecutory laws were nullified by different emperors at different times, but Constantine and Licinius's Edict of Milan (313) has traditionally marked the end of the persecution.

Christians had always been subject to local discrimination in the empire, but early emperors were reluctant to issue general laws against them. It was not until the 250s, under the reigns of Decius and Valerian, that such laws were passed. Under this legislation, Christians were compelled to sacrifice to pagan gods or face imprisonment and execution. After Gallienus's accession in 260, these laws went into abeyance. Diocletian's accession in 284 did not mark an immediate reversal of disregard to Christianity, but it did herald a gradual shift in official attitudes toward religious minorities. In the first fifteen years of his rule, Diocletian purged the army of Christians, condemned Manicheans to death, and surrounded himself with public opponents of Christianity. Diocletian's preference for activist government, combined with his self-image as a restorer of past Roman glory, presaged the most pervasive persecution in Roman history. In the winter of 302, Galerius urged Diocletian to begin a general persecution of the Christians. Diocletian was wary, and asked the oracle of Apollo for guidance. The oracle's reply was read as an endorsement of Galerius's position, and a general persecution was called on February 24, 303.

Persecutory policies varied in intensity across the empire. Where Galerius and Diocletian were avid persecutors, Constantius was unenthusiastic. Later persecutory edicts, including the calls for universal sacrifice, were not applied in his domain. His son, Constantine, on taking the imperial office in 306, restored Christians to full legal equality and returned property that had been confiscated during the persecution. In Italy in 306, the usurper Maxentius ousted Maximian's successor Severus, promising full religious toleration. Galerius ended the persecution in the East in 311, but it was resumed in Egypt, Palestine, and Asia Minor by his successor, Maximinus. Constantine and Licinius, Severus's successor, signed the "Edict of Milan" in 313, which offered a more comprehensive acceptance of Christianity than Galerius's edict had provided. Licinius ousted Maximinus in 313, bringing an end to persecution in the East.

The persecution failed to check the rise of the church. By 324, Constantine was sole ruler of the empire, and Christianity had become his favored religion. Although the persecution resulted in the deaths of—according to one modern estimate—3,000 Christians, and the torture, imprisonment, or dislocation of many more, most Christians avoided punishment. The persecution did, however, cause many churches to split between those who had complied with imperial authority (the traditores), and those who had remained "pure." Certain schisms, like those of the Donatists in North Africa and the Meletians in Egypt, persisted long after the persecutions. The Donatists would not be reconciled to the Catholic Church until after 411. These accounts were criticized during the Enlightenment and after, most notably by Edward Gibbon. Modern historians like G. E. M. de Ste. Croix have attempted to determine whether Christian sources exaggerated the scope of the Diocletianic persecution.

## Persecution of Christians by Christians

In the Eastern Roman Empire Emperors were established as both Orthodox and Arian as Constantine's own sons Constantius II, Constantine II (who proceeded Constantine I) were Arian. Later still, the Emperor Valens also was an Arian. The Germanic Goths and Vandals adhered to Arian Christianity, establishing Arian states in Italy and Spain. Orthodox Christians defended themselves vigorously against these foreign Arians. In 429 the Vandals (who were Arians) conquered Roman Africa. Catholics were discriminated against; Church property was confiscated. Thousands of Catholics were banished from Vandal held territory. St. Augustine, for example, died while in a town besieged by the Arian Vandals. As it was the fall of Rome to the Goths, tribes who throughout their histories were a mix of Pagan and Arian Christians.

In the medieval period the Roman Catholic Church moved to suppress the Cathar heresy, the Pope having sanctioned a crusade against the Albigensians; during the course of which the massacre of Beziers took place, with between seven and twenty thousand deaths. (This was the occasion when the papal legate, Arnaud Amalric, asked about how Catholics could be distinguished from Cathars once the city fell, famously replied, "Kill them all, God will know His own."). Over the twenty-year period of this campaign an estimated 200,000 to 1,000,000 people were killed. John Huss, a Bohemian preacher of reformation, was burned at the stake on July 6, 1415. Pope Martin V issued a bull on 17 March 1420 which proclaimed a crusade "for the destruction of the Wycliffites, Hussites and all other heretics in Bohemia."

The Crusades in the Middle East also spilled over into conquest of Eastern Orthodox Christians by Roman Catholics and attempted suppression of the Orthodox Church. The Waldenses were as well persecuted by the Catholic Church, but survive up to this day. The Reformation led to a long period of warfare and communal violence between Catholic and Protestant factions, leading to massacres and forced suppression of the alternative views by the dominant faction in many countries. In the 1572 St. Bartholomew's Day Massacre the French king ordered the murder of Protestants in France.

Intolerance of dissident forms of Protestantism continued, as evidenced by the exodus of the Pilgrims who sought refuge in America, founding the Plymouth Colony in Massachusetts in 1620. In the modern period, such events include violence between Mormons and Protestants in the United States during the 19th century. That century also saw the alleged martyrdom of St. Peter the Aleut at the hands of Roman Catholic clergy in San Francisco, California.

Anti-Catholicism officially began in 1534 during the English Reformation; the Act of Supremacy made the King of England the "only supreme head on earth of the Church in England." Any act of allegiance to the latter was considered treason. It was under this act that Thomas More was executed. Queen Elizabeth I's scorn for Jesuit missionaries led to many executions at Tyburn. As punishment for the rebellion of 1641, almost all lands owned by Irish Catholics were confiscated and given to Protestant settlers. Under the penal laws no Irish Catholic could sit in the Parliament of Ireland, even though some 90% of Ireland's population was native Irish Catholic when the first of these bans was introduced in 1691. Catholic/Protestant strife has been blamed for much of "The Troubles," the ongoing struggle in Northern Ireland.

This attitude was carried to the American colonies, which would leave England, forming the United States. In the English colonies, Catholicism was introduced with the settling of Maryland in 1634; this colony offered a rare example of religious toleration in a fairly intolerant age, particularly amongst other English colonies which frequently exhibited a quite militant Protestantism. (See the Maryland Toleration Act, and note the pre-eminence of the Archdiocese of Baltimore in Catholic circles.) However, at the time of the American Revolution, Catholics formed less than 1% of the population of the thirteen colonies.

Although there has been a strong anti-Catholic sentiment in North America since before the dawn of the US, the feeling grew stronger during waves of Catholic immigration from old Europe. These huge numbers of immigrant Catholics came from Ireland, Southern Germany, Italy, Poland and Eastern Europe. Nationalist, nativist feeling was represented by the Know-Nothing Party. Father James Coyle, a Roman Catholic priest, was murdered in 1921 by the Ku Klux Klan.

Anti-Protestantism originated in a reaction by the Catholic Church against the Protestant Reformation of the 16th century. Protestants were denounced as heretics and subject to persecution in those territories, such as Spain, Italy and the Netherlands, in which the Catholics were the dominant power. This movement was orchestrated by Popes and Princes as the Counter Reformation. This resulted in religious wars and eruptions of sectarian hatred such as the St. Bartholomew's Day Massacre.

When the disputes between Lutherans and Roman Catholics gained a political dimension, both groups saw other groups of religious dissidents that were arising as a danger to their own security. The early "Täufer" (lit. "Baptists") were mistrusted and rejected by both religio-political parties. Religious persecution is often perpetrated as a means of political control, and this becomes evident with the Treaty of Augsburg in 1555. This treaty provided the legal groundwork for persecution of the Anabaptists.

## Persecutions of Early Christians Outside the Roman Empire

In 341, Shapur II ordered the massacre of all Christians in Persia. During the persecution, about 1,150 Christians were martyred under Shapur II. In the 4th century, the Terving King Athanaric began persecuting Christians, many of whom were killed.

## Examples of Muslim Persecution of Christians

### Republic of Turkey

In modern Turkey, the Istanbul pogrom was a state-sponsored and state-orchestrated pogrom that compelled Greek Christians to leave Istanbul the first Christian city in violation to the Treaty of Lausanne. The issue of Christian genocides by the Turks may become a problem, since Turkey wishes to join the European Union.

### Sudan

In Sudan, it is estimated that over 1.5 million Christians have been killed by the Janjaweed, the Arab Muslim militia, and even suspected Islamists in northern Sudan since 1984. It should also be noted that Sudan's several civil wars (which often take the form of genocidal campaigns) are often not only purely religious in nature, but also ethnic, as many black Muslims, as well as Muslim Arab tribesmen, have also been killed in the conflicts.

It is estimated that as many as 200,000 people had been taken into slavery during the Second Sudanese Civil War. The slaves are mostly Dinka people.

## Pakistan

In Pakistan 1.5% of the population are Christian. Pakistani law mandates that "blasphemies" of the Qur'an are to be met with punishment. Ayub Masih, a Christian, was convicted of blasphemy and sentenced to death in 1998. He was accused by a neighbor of stating that he supported British writer, Salman Rushdie, author of *The Satanic Verses*. Lower appeals courts upheld the conviction. However, before the Pakistan Supreme Court, his lawyer was able to prove that the accuser had used the conviction to force Masih's family off their land and then acquired control of the property. Masih has been released. The Christian community in Pakistan is the target of attacks by Islamic extremists. In October 2001, gunmen on motorcycles opened fire on a Protestant congregation in the Punjab, killing 18 people. In March 2002 five people were killed in an attack on a church in Islamabad, including an American schoolgirl and her mother. In August 2002, masked gunmen stormed a Christian missionary school for foreigners in Islamabad; six people were killed and three injured. None of those killed were children of foreign missionaries. In August 2002, grenades were thrown at a church in the grounds of a Christian hospital in northwest Pakistan, near Islamabad, killing three nurses. On September 25, 2002, two terrorists entered the "Peace and Justice Institute," Karachi, where they separated Muslims from the Christians, and then murdered seven Christians by shooting them in the head. All of the victims were Pakistani Christians. Karachi police chief Tariq Jamil said the victims had their hands tied and their mouths had been covered with tape. In December 2002, three young girls were blown apart when hand grenade was thrown into a church near Lahore on Christmas Day.

In November 2005 3,000 militant Islamists attacked Christians in Sangla Hill in Pakistan and destroyed Roman Catholic, Salvation Army and United Presbyterian churches. The attack was over allegations of violation of blasphemy laws by a Pakistani Christian named Yousaf Masih. On June 5, 2006, a Pakistani Christian stonemason, Nasir Ashraf, was working near Lahore when he drank water from a public facility using a glass chained to the facility. He was assaulted by Muslims for "Polluting the glass." A mob developed, who beat Ashraf, calling him a "Christian dog." Bystanders encouraged the beating and joined in. Ashraf was eventually hospitalized. One year later, in August 2007, a Christian missionary couple, Rev. Arif and Kathleen Khan, were gunned down by militant Islamists in Islamabad. The "official" position in Pakistan is that the killer was a fellow Christian, and that the killings were "justified" as an honor killing under the false pretext that the missionaries were engaged in sexual harassment, an assertion widely doubted in the international media, as well as by Pakistani Christians. In August 2009 six Christians including 4 women and a child were burnt alive by Muslim militants and a church set ablaze in Gojra, Pakistan, when violence broke out after alleged desecration of the Qu'ran.

## Egypt

While the Egyptian government does not have a policy to persecute Christians, it discriminates against them and hampers their freedom of worship. Its agencies sporadically persecute Muslim converts to Christianity. The government enforces Hamayouni Decree restrictions on building or repairing churches. These same restrictions, however, do not apply to mosques.

The government has effectively restricted Christians from senior government, diplomatic, military, and educational positions, and there has been increasing discrimination in the private sector. The government subsidizes media which attack Christianity and restricts Christians access to the state-controlled media.

In Egypt the government does not officially recognize conversions from Islam to Christianity; because certain interfaith marriages are not allowed either, this prevents marriages between converts to Christianity and those born in Christian communities, and also results in the children of Christian converts being classified as Muslims and given a Muslim education. The government also applies religiously discriminatory laws and practices concerning clergy salaries.

Foreign missionaries are allowed in the country only if they restrict their activities to social improvements and refrain from proselytizing. The Coptic Pope Shenouda III was internally exiled in 1981 by President Anwar Sadat, who then chose five Coptic bishops and asked them to choose a new pope. They refused, and in 1985 President Hosni Mubarak restored Pope Shenouda III, who had been accused of fomenting interconfessional strife. Particularly in Upper Egypt, the rise in extremist Islamist groups such as the Gama'at Islamiya during the 1980s was accompanied by attacks on Copts and on Coptic churches; these have since declined with the decline of those organizations, but still continue. The police have been accused of siding with the attackers in some of these cases.

Many colleges dictate quotas for Coptic students, often around 1 or 2% despite the group making up 15% of the country's population. There is also a separate tax-funded education system called Al Azhar, catering to students from elementary to college level, which accepts no Christian Coptic students, teachers or administrators.

Hundreds of Christian Coptic girls have been kidnapped and forcibly converted to Islam, as well as being victims of rape and forced marriage to Muslim men.

In April 2006, one person was killed and twelve injured in simultaneous knife attacks on three Coptic churches in Alexandria.

In November 2008, several thousand Muslims attacked a Coptic church in a suburb of Cairo on the day of its inauguration, forcing 800 Coptic Christians to barricade themselves in.

On September 18, 2009, a Muslim man called Osama Araban beheaded a Coptic Christian man in the village of Bagour, and injured 2 others in 2 different villages. He was arrested the following day.

## Saudi Arabia

Saudi Arabia is an Islamic state that practices Wahhabism and restricts all other religions, including the possession of religious items such as the Bible, crucifixes, and Stars of David. Christians are arrested and lashed in public for practicing their faith openly. Strict Sharia is enforced. Muslims are forbidden to convert to another religion. If one does so and does not recant, they may be executed.

## In other Muslim nations

Though Iran recognizes Assyrian and Armenian Christians as a religious minority (along with Jews and Zoroastrians) and they have representatives in the Parliament, after the 1979 Revolution, Muslim converts to Christianity (typically to Protestant Christianity) have been arrested and sometimes executed.

In the Philippines, the Moro Islamic Liberation Front and Abu Sayyaf has attacked and killed Christians.

In Indonesia, religious conflicts have typically occurred in Western New Guinea, Maluku (particularly Ambon), and Sulawesi. The presence of Muslims in these regions is in part a result of the transmigrasi program of population re-distribution. Conflicts have often occurred because of the aims of radical Islamist organizations such as Jemaah Islamiah or Laskar Jihad to impose Sharia, with such groups attacking Christians and destroying over 600 churches. In 2006 three Christian girls were beheaded as retaliation for previous Muslim deaths in Christian-Muslim rioting. The men were imprisoned for the murders, including Jemaah Islamiyah's district ringleader Hasanuddin. On going to jail, Hasanuddin said, "It's not a problem (if I am being sentenced to prison), because this is a part of our struggle."

In Afghanistan, Abdul Rahman, a 41-year-old citizen, was charged in 2006 with rejecting Islam a crime punishable by death under Sharia law. He has since been released into exile in the West under intense pressure from Western governments. In 2008, the Taliban killed a British charity worker, Gayle Williams, for being a Christian.

In Kosovo, since June 1999, 156 churches and monasteries have been damaged or destroyed and several priests have been killed. During the few days of the 2004 unrest in Kosovo, 35 churches and monasteries were damaged and some destroyed by Muslim mobs.

In Malaysia, although Islam is the official religion, Christianity is mostly tolerated, however, in order to be a member of the majority race (the Malays, one is legally required to be a Muslim. Also, if a non-Muslim marries a Muslim, they are legally required to convert to Islam. There is much debate over whether Malaysia is a liberal Islamic state or a very religious secular state. In 2002, a currently unidentified gunman killed Bonnie Penner Witherall at a prenatal clinic in Sidon, Lebanon. She had been proselytizing and attempting to convert Muslims to Christianity. Three Christian missionaries were killed in their hospital in Jibla, Yemen, in December 2002. A gunman, apprehended by the authorities, said that he did it "for his religion."

# STORIES GIVEN for OUR LEARNING

As we seek to become an apostolic, overcoming church that stands for truth in the face of persecution, we will often find it necessary to look to God for guidance and hope. God has provided exactly what we need, as He shows us in the promise of Romans 15:4:

> For everything that was written in the past was written to teach us, so that through endurance and the encouragement of the Scriptures we might have hope.

The Old Testament tells us stories about great leaders like Abraham, Moses, and David. We often tell these stories to the children in Sunday school and then forget that they are truth with divine principles, given for our learning so that we will not repeat the same mistakes others have made. One important principle we can learn from Abraham, Moses, and David is that God's chosen ones never were perfect. They never had an easy life. Sometimes God's choice of leaders seems strange. People see the weaknesses of their leaders and judge what they see, but God sees more. He sees deeper and makes His choices separate from people's judgment.

## Abraham

> When Abram was ninety-nine years old, the LORD appeared to him and said, "I am God Almighty; walk before me and be blameless. I will confirm my covenant between me and you and will greatly increase your numbers."
>
> —GENESIS 17:1–2

God chose Abraham to become the father of nations, and He stood faithfully by His Word, even though Abraham was imperfect and made mistakes. Somehow God looks through our imperfection and right into our hearts to deal with us in His own way.

One example of Abraham's weakness may be seen in Genesis 16, where he tried to get God's promise of a son on his own. The result was Ishmael, and the offspring from Ishmael are the enemies of Israel today. This was certainly not a blameless act by Abraham.

The Bible also shows how Abraham had a big problem with fear and did another act that was not blameless:

> Now Abraham moved on from there into the region of the Negev and lived between Kadesh and Shur. For a while he stayed in Gerar, and there Abraham said of his wife Sarah, "She is my sister." Then Abimelech king of Gerar sent for Sarah and took her. But God came to Abimelech in a dream one night and said to him, "You are as good as dead because of the woman you have taken; she is a married woman"....Then Abimelech called Abraham in and said, "What have you done to us? How have I wronged you that you have brought such great guilt upon me and my kingdom? You have done things to me that should not be done." And Abimelech asked Abraham, "What was your reason for doing this?" Abraham replied, "I said to myself, 'There is surely no fear of God in this place, and they will kill me because of my wife.'"
> —Genesis 20:1–3, 9–11

In spite of Abraham's imperfections, God stood true to His word and fulfilled His promises to him.

## Moses

Moses is described in Numbers 12:3 as the meekest—most "gentle, kind and humble" (AMP)—man on Earth. He did great things, leading Israel out of Egypt and performing many miracles. God appeared to him in a burning bush, and he saw God face to face on Mount Sinai. Yet, Moses was far from being a perfect leader figure.

Since Moses could not speak well, God gave him his brother, Aaron, to speak for him. Moses had a problem with anger, and Numbers 20:7–12 tells how he hit the rock instead of speaking to it, as God commanded him. Because of his disobedience, he was not allowed to take Israel into the Promised Land. Moses was also a murderer, but nevertheless, he was God's man! Many times the children of Israel wanted to kill him, stone him, leave him, or betray him; but, Moses still was God's chosen one!

## David

David is well known as a man after God's heart. He was the chosen king, and yet, he was far from perfect. He had a problem with women, something that his son Solomon inherited. In fact, it became the cause of Solomon's fall at the end of his reign. David committed adultery and murdered a man to hide his sin. He only repented when he was pushed against the wall by the prophet Nathan. Yet, God not only allowed him to remain king after he committed all these sins, but He also blessed and rewarded him.

## The Principle of God's Forgiveness and Judgment

God is, has always been, and always will be. God never changes, and the way He deals with people and their sin never changes. He forgives when we repent and forgets that we even sinned. If there is no repentance, however, God will not let anyone get by with it. For example, God killed all mankind except Noah and his family when He judged the world with a flood.

If you read the Bible carefully, God's principles of repentance and forgiveness of sins worked for everyone's salvation and safety in the Bible who took it to heart and acted according to it. And the same principles always worked in my life since I have become a born again and Spirit-filled Christian.

However, people usually choose captivity and curses instead of repentance, obedience, and blessing. The Old Testament shows how God allowed the children of Israel to be taken captive by their enemies. As soon they had a king who led them into repentance, He delivered them. God always chose a leader like Moses to lead Israel into freedom, and His people always disobeyed.

If God has dealt with people this way in the Bible and throughout history, what makes us think that He will close His eyes to all the sin the church is committing today? I am convinced that the takeover of Europe by Islam is the judgment of God on that continent. For so long Europe has resisted God and rejected Him, and in all its pride it is being blinded by embracing Islam.

However, we do not have to repeat the mistakes that gave way to the Nazi Holocaust carried out on the Jews if we will learn the divine principles God has given us. The Bible gives us all the answers we need. This may sound simply foolish, but defeating the devil by dying on the cross and being resurrected after three days sounds foolish too. Still, it remains the only truth!

The Bible says in Psalm 146:8:

> The LORD gives sight to the blind, the LORD lifts up those who are bowed down, the LORD loves the righteous.

My prayer is that God will open our eyes and raise us up as sons and daughters of God to stand against the evil of Islam. The Lord opens our eyes to this calling of God, and I cannot convince you if you are not open. However, I can urge you to look at the difference between Jesus, the living Word of God, and the Quran. Mohammed said in Surah 4:168:

> Those who disbelieve and deal in wrong, Allah will never forgive. He will never forgive them, neither will he guide them onto a road.

Islam is an oppressive religion that does not raise people up but rather pushes them down. However, our message is the message of the Bible, the gospel of forgiveness. When we do wrong and are on the wrong road, we can turn to God and receive His forgiveness. It is a message, just like our T-shirts say, that Jesus is only one way to be saved. It is a message of life and justice. Our message is also a political message in the sense that we are against the political system of Islam and the laws that radical Muslims are trying to force upon our society.

Islam is not a religion; it is a religious political system. I am convinced that God allowed Islam to be manifested in Europe so strongly because of the lack of repentance of the churches in Europe's countries throughout history. God gave Europe over to the demonic evil of Islam, and unless there is repentance, Europe has to suffer that punishment. If we in the United States of America are not careful, the same punishment will await us. In the UK some churches came together and pressured the government to ban Westboro Baptist church members (a radical church, who speak up against the sins in the churches and warns them before the judgment of God) from entering the country.

> An alliance of six UK religious groups (the Baptist Union of Great Britain, Evangelical Alliance UK, Faithworks, Methodist Church of Great Britain, United Reformed Church and Bible Society-funded think-tank Theos) made a joint statement on February 19, 2009, in support of the government's decision and condemning the activities of the Westboro Baptist Church saying, "We do not share [Westboro's] hatred of lesbian and gay people. We believe that God loves all, irrespective of sexual orientation, and we unreservedly stand against their message of hate toward those communities."[1]

Germany's chancellor Merkel traveled to the Maledives, after being invited to help them to islamisize their country.[2] As long as Europe's churches will judge and are not standing up against the kind of political decisions that open doors to the wrong side, God cannot help them. God will not send his chosen leaders of our time to lead Europe out of a huge captivity and oppression called Islam that is heading its way.

## God's Chosen Ones Were Never Perfect

God has always chosen leaders to lead his folk. God's chosen men were not perfect, and it was never a problem for God. In general people today do not tolerate or even forgive weaknesses in leaders. Weaknesses are used to tear those leaders apart, if it fits the purpose. I have experienced through the years that as soon as a leader is not giving the people what they want, his weaknesses will become a weapon against him. As we just read about David, God forgave David's sins and confirmed him as king. In today's church I am sure David would have been forced to give up his leadership position. We need to see how important it is to repent and forgive. In Europe's history we find the Catholic Church dominated for many decades. People suffered a lot under its controlling power.

The Catholic Church at that time was hiding the truth of the Bible from the common people. The services were held in Latin so only the educated people could understand the Word of God and the plain folks could be held in bondage. It was common for the people at that time to pay the church for their eternal life.

Martin Luther brought back the revelation of salvation and justification by faith, and the Bible was translated for the common people. Luther withstood the pressure of the Catholic Church and their entire system. Risking his life, he rebelled against them and founded a new movement—Protestantism. (This is a branch within Christianity that contains many denominations with differing practices and doctrines. It principally originated in the sixteenth-century Protestant Reformation, begun with his *Ninety-five Theses* in 1517.)

> His translation of the Bible into the language of the people (instead of Latin) made it more accessible, causing a tremendous impact on the church and on German culture. It fostered the development of a standard version of the German language, added several principles to the art of translation, and influenced the translation into English of the King James Bible. His hymns inspired the development of singing in churches. His marriage to Katharina von Bora set a model for the practice of clerical marriage, allowing Protestant priests to marry.
>
> Much scholarly debate has focused on Luther's writings about the Jews. His statements that the Jews' homes should be destroyed, their synagogues burned, money confiscated, and liberty curtailed were revived and used in propaganda by the Nazis from 1933 to 1945.[1]

Luther's stand against the Jews and his fight against the Catholic Church opened the doors to compromise concerning the tolerance of Islam.

> At the time of the Marburg Colloquy, Suleiman the Magnificent was besieging Vienna with a vast Ottoman army. Luther had argued against resisting the Turks in his 1518 Explanation of the Ninety-five Theses,

provoking accusations of defeatism. He saw the Turks as a scourge sent to punish Christians by God, as agents of the biblical apocalypse that would destroy the antichrist, whom Luther believed to be the papacy, and the Roman Church. He consistently rejected the idea of a Holy War, "as though our people were an army of Christians against the Turks, who were enemies of Christ. This is absolutely contrary to Christ's doctrine and name". On the other hand, in keeping with his doctrine of the two kingdoms, Luther did support non-religious war against the Turks. In 1526, he argued in Whether Soldiers can be in a State of Grace that national defence is reason for a just war. By 1529, in On War against the Turk, he was actively urging Emperor Charles V and the German people to fight a secular war against the Turks. He made clear, however, that the spiritual war against an alien faith was separate, to be waged through prayer and repentance. Around the time of the Siege of Vienna, Luther wrote a prayer for national deliverance from the Turks, asking God to "give to our emperor perpetual victory over our enemies."

In 1542, Luther read a Latin translation of the Qur'an. He went on to produce several critical pamphlets on the Islamic faith, which he called Mohammedanism or the Turk. Though Luther saw the Muslim faith as a tool of the devil, he was indifferent to its practice: "Let the Turk believe and live as he will, just as one lets the papacy and other false Christians live." He opposed banning the publication of the Qur'an, wanting it exposed to scrutiny.[2]

With the foundation of the Protestantism a door was opened from what was considered the one and only valid church, the Roman Catholic Empire, to churches of all forms of doctrine and theology. It is amazing what a difference just one man can make, if he is deeply convinced.

> Protestantism is a branch within Christianity, containing many denominations with some differing practices and doctrines, that principally originated in the sixteenth-century Protestant Reformation. It is considered to be one of the major divisions within Christianity, together with the Roman Catholic, Eastern Orthodox, Oriental Orthodox and Anglican traditions. Some groups that are often loosely labeled "Protestant" do not use the term to define themselves and some tend to reject it because of the implication of being non-traditional. Anglicanism, for instance, which gained much of its distinctive identity during and immediately following the English Reformation, is viewed by many of its adherents as not having its origins in the Reformation but as a "Reformed Catholic" tradition. Likewise, many Baptists and Pentecostals do not see themselves as descended from 16th-century Protestant movements. As such, the term

Protestantism is often used loosely to denote all non-Roman Catholic varieties of Western Christianity, rather than to denote those churches adhering to the principles described below.

Protestantism is associated with the doctrine of sola scriptura, which maintains that the Bible (rather than church tradition or ecclesiastical interpretations of the Bible) is the final source of authority for all Christians. Another distinctive Protestant doctrine is that of sola fide, which holds that faith alone, rather than good works, is sufficient for the salvation of the believer.

Protestant churches tend not to accept the Catholic and Orthodox doctrine of apostolic succession and associated ideas regarding the sacramental ministry of the clergy, though there are some exceptions to this. Protestant ministers and church leaders therefore generally play a somewhat different role in their communities than Catholic and Orthodox priests and bishops.

Protestantism has both conservative and liberal theological strands within it. Protestant styles of public worship tend to be simpler and less elaborate than those of Roman Catholics, Anglicans, and Eastern Christians, sometimes radically so, though there are exceptions to this tendency.

Examples of denominations within Protestantism include Lutheranism, Calvinism (including both Reformed churches and Presbyterianism), Methodism, the Baptist churches, and the Seventh-day Adventist Church.[3]

With Martin Luther the revelation of salvation by faith was released by God again. Luther was used in a great way by God in this one aspect, but because of judging and unforgiveness toward the Catholic Church, he made so many terrible mistakes. Martin Luther took the right of judgment into his own hands because he received one revelation from God. With this action he opened a spiritual door for rebellion and revolution not only coming into the church but into the European nations. Luther opened another door to evil as he compromised with the Turks in order to be more successful in his fight against the Catholic Church and the Jews. He compromised with Islam! The curse of this compromise is all over Europe today. It is interesting that the Christian Church and the Jews are now defending the right for freedom for Islam in Europe! Disobedience to God's Word brings a curse on the land. Unless there is true repentance the curse will remain and linger.

We suffer under Martin Luther's mistakes still today. Instead of leaving the Catholic Church to God, he wanted it to be destroyed. He considered her to be the Antichrist. He was persecuting and destroying not only the Catholic Church, but the Jews as well. You do not touch God's chosen, whether it is a nation or a church or a man. No matter how right or wrong those people are, you do not touch them; you leave them to God.

Before Luther's Reformation there was only one church. After the Reformation churches of all kinds of backgrounds and beliefs came in existence. Each time a new church with a new revelation was born, it was persecuted by the old. The persecution was so hard that in the eighteenth century certain people decided to leave Europe and go to America to escape the persecution and to have religious freedom. This is why a new nation was founded: one nation under God, the United States of America! It is the land of the free, the home of the brave!

But, where are the brave? Where are the free? With time America started to repeat the same mistakes.

# The CHURCH and the GOVERNMENT

True Christianity is not open-minded. It strongly declares that there was, is, and always will be only one way to be saved and forgiven. There is only one way to come to the Father, and that is through Jesus Christ, the Son of God, alone. We proclaim this message on the sign in our church yard, not to offend or spread any kind of hatred but to raise awareness of the truth. We want to shock all people to think about this truth, and we especially want to motivate Christians to support it.

We were very disappointed that more Christians and pastors in our community would not stand up and say, "Yes, the essence, the message, on the sign is true. There is only one message that comes from God: Jesus Christ is the only way. Any other message comes from below, from the devil."

## Our Freedom Is in Danger

When Christians are not willing to stand up for their beliefs, we cannot hope that the government will protect the church. In the Old Testament we read that God's plan was to lead the children of Israel through the voice of the prophets. God used the prophets to speak to His people, but He Himself wanted to be the government for His people. However, the children of Israel rejected God's way of ruling and reigning, and they longed for a king, just like the other nations. They wanted to be like everyone else. They could not see how special and unique and privileged they were, and they became ungrateful for all God had done for them.

This is a lot like what happened with America. The development in the United States is moving away from God more and more. During his term, the people were rejecting President Bush. Statistics say that he was the most unpopular president in U.S. history.[1] It is interesting that he was a Spirit-filled believer, a man full of the fear of the Lord. He made decisions after what he thought was right. Those kinds of people are not popular!

Now we have a president who claims to be Christian but stands for abortion and same-sex marriage. There was a euphoria about President Obama, who appeared out of nowhere and was celebrated worldwide as an idol! Few people had ever heard of him before the elections. He had accomplished nothing. He had little experience in politics. Yet, he has already received the Nobel Prize—for just being popular. Wake up, America! Wake up! The American people rejected God, and God gave them what they wanted so badly: a man who just wants to please the people to get reelected, just like the church leaders and pastors of our time today.

God gave Israel a king, beginning with the reign of King Saul and of King David. This was to their ruin, and the people of Israel eventually ended up in captivity. God allowed them to be taken captive because there was no other way to break through to them about their need to humble themselves and repent. In their captivity the people started to cry out to their God again, and God saved them. Maybe we are standing right before a change of times.

Governments change, and the laws change with them. Today the law might protect the church; tomorrow the law could kill the church. This process has already started with the action of taking the Ten Commandments out of the courthouses. Students are restricted about how they may evangelize in school. When our church evangelizes on the streets or in public areas, people call the police on us. A man was fired from his job for wearing a button that said "One nation under God."[2] People who speak out against homosexuality in the workplace are fired.

When our people were on their way to do some grocery shopping, the police approached them because they were wearing our T-shirts with the message "Islam is of the devil." The police said, "Take off your shirt," and our people answered, "Why? Is it against the law?" The police responded, "No, but it offends people." Our people, of course, did not take their shirts off, but how long can we walk in freedom? As governments change and protect the wrong things, our freedom is in danger.

## When God Is Removed from Government

The intellectual and humanistic world has the goal of complete separation of government and religion. The reason for this—and it is understandably good—is that governments have historically used religion to oppress and control people. Christians and churches feel controlled by true apostolic ministry and anointing, and they reject this most important gift from God. This fear is proof of the absence of God. It is driving people to seek control of their circumstances instead of trusting and believing God. And if we reject God, He cannot lead, help, or save us!

Fear of being controlled dominates the entire European continent, and it is bringing the people under the control of Islam. When people try very hard to fight the control of religion, they open the door to it. The Bible teaches this when it says in Proverbs 10:24:

> The thing a wicked man fears shall come upon him, but the desire of the [uncompromisingly] righteous shall be granted. (AMP)

I spent more than thirty years in Germany, where Christian humanism would be a good description of the church and where Islam seems to be taking over. The conditions are worse in the United Kingdom.

In Europe God has been removed from the government completely. It is like the description the Book of Nehemiah gives about Jerusalem, the city of God, which was unprotected because its walls were destroyed. God sent Nehemiah to rebuild the walls, and he found men who were willing to pay the price and help him as long as it took to complete the work. In a similar way, the church God used me to build in Cologne, Germany, was called to rebuild the walls and restore the presence of God in that nation. However, it failed, because there were no men willing to pay the price and finish the work.

Islam has once again proved itself to be a terrible, perverted, violent religion. Faleh Almaleki, an Iraqi Muslim, intentionally hit his twenty-year-old daughter, Noor, with his car in late 2009. He thought his daughter had become too Westernized, so he ran over her and her boyfriend's mom as they were walking through a parking lot. Faleh was charged with aggravated assault for his crime, but his daughter's life was cut short.[3] She will never marry and have children. She will never have a future, a chance to be saved and experience the mercy of God by trusting in Jesus. Her own father took her life, and under Islamic law he is justified. Governments change, and with them the laws change.

Not long after this incident, another horrible thing happened right in the heart of our nation in our military on our own soil. On November 5, 2009, a Muslim U. S. army psychiatrist in Fort Hood, Texas, walked into a military complex, shouted out in Arabic, "God is great," and then killed thirteen American soldiers and wounded thirty others.[4] Islam has come to America, and it is trying to promote its perverted laws and violence here. This man, Major Nadal Malik Hasan, thought he was doing a good thing, upholding the laws of Allah. The Islamic law teaches "fighting is proscribed for you" (Surah 2:216) and "slay the idolaters wherever you find them" (Surah 9:5).

If radical Muslims are able to infiltrate the military and over a period of time fool everyone to such an extent that they can do such a terrible act, does that not show where we are in this nation? Does it not say that we, the church, have to stand up and do something? The government failed, and the military failed! If the church fails too, there will be no hope left!

In Christianity our nature is to forgive, to give a second chance. The Quran says, "Fight those who believe not in Allah" (Surah 9:29). Radical Muslims have a goal, a vision, a plan. They are not worried about what some other people said. Omar Ahmad, the founder of the Council of American-Islamic Relations (CAIR), said in a controversial interview:

> Islam isn't in America to be equal to any other religion, but to become dominant. The Koran, the Muslim book of scripture, should be the highest authority in America, and Islam the only accepted religion on Earth.[5]

That is what Islam proclaims, and we in the church are called to respond to it. We must stop it, or it will not be stopped. If we do not, we will have a new government where killing is the right thing to do. We cannot wait for the government to save us from it, and we cannot rely on the army. We just saw how Islam is already in the army!

When we examine today's generation of youth, we see mega problems with people having an undisciplined lifestyle. Obesity and immorality are common and accepted, to name a couple concerns. I just read a report that 75 percent of America's youth are not able to pass the qualifying examination for the army, because they do not meet the requirements for intelligence or weight or they have been in trouble with the law.[6] That is disgraceful, and it takes the power out of our army! It reflects again the shape of today's church: too fat, too lazy, too undisciplined! If you teach discipline in the church today, the people run off to the church around the corner. You will be labeled as a controlling church!

In addition, we cannot forget the curse that has come upon us because we allow thousands of unborn children to be killed legally every day. We must speak out. The church must stand up and speak out. The Bible says in Proverbs 20:13:

> Do not love sleep or you will grow poor; stay awake and you will have food to spare.

We in the church have become poor because we love sleep. What is sleep (in this context)? Sleep is a state of denial. It is closing our eyes and not wanting to be involved. Sleep is a state of being passive and doing nothing. This is the state of the church. The church has become blind, and it wants to be blind. It only wants to lie down and escape any action and recognition. And as the church is lying down, the rest of the world—and especially Islam—is running over us.

It is time for our politicians, and more so for our churches, to open our eyes and see that we are losing the battle. We are not gaining ground, but instead we are hiding in the hills. Our churches are full of cowards, and they are being led by cowards, pastors who would rather please the people than God. In that aspect, we must learn from Islam. In Islam the desire is to please its perverted god, called Allah. We must return to wanting to please God, to do what we are called to do. We must change and influence the society.

## The Goliath of Our Time

First Samuel 17 tells how the Philistine army had a champion, a giant named Goliath. This giant challenged King Saul and the Israelite army every day for forty days, asking them to choose a man who would come and fight him. The Israelites were afraid of Goliath, but young David, who had come to visit his three oldest brothers at the site of the battle, was not. When he heard Goliath defy the army of Israel, he stepped forward to go and fight the giant. With five smooth stones and his sling in his hand, David approached Goliath and said:

> David said to the Philistine, "You come against me with sword and spear and javelin, but I come against you in the name of the LORD Almighty, the God of the armies of Israel, whom you have defied. This day the LORD will hand you over to me, and I'll strike you down and cut off your head. Today I will give the carcasses of the Philistine army to the birds of the air and the beasts of the earth, and the whole world will know that there is a God in Israel. All those gathered here will know that it is not by sword or spear that the LORD saves; for the battle is the LORD's, and he will give all of you into our hands."
> —1 SAMUEL 17:45–47

David took one stone, slung it, and struck Goliath on the forehead, causing him to fall facedown on the ground. Taking Goliath's sword, David killed the giant, and Israel won a great victory over the Philistines as they fled after their champion had fallen. It all happened because David believed God and took action against the enemy.

Islam is the Goliath of our time, and it is coming out to challenge the world. It is mocking Christians and their God, and the church is hiding, cowardly, in the hills, hoping that this Goliath will simply disappear. The governments on Earth are like Saul, who was unable to face the challenge, fight for freedom, and overcome the enemy. David, the teenage boy who killed Goliath, is a picture of the overcoming church of today! He faced the challenge bravely and overcame the giant with one stone and his trust in God.

David was the eighth son, the one who was taking care of the sheep when the prophet Samuel came to anoint the new king. Not even David's own father believed in him when it came to God and the kingdom. Still David was the chosen and anointed one, God's man, and because he humbled himself and was obedient to God, he overcame the giant.

It takes only one person, one church—usually one no one would have chosen—to stand up and fight against the enemy! It may be the one everyone is rejecting and despising, maybe a church like Dove World Outreach Center. We can't count the times people (including close friends and family), media, or government officials have tried to come against us and destroy our ministry. David was persecuted by his own family and Saul, who represented the government. He had to live in the land of his enemies to survive and wait until his time came to be king.

Without David stepping out and facing the challenge against the fearful attitude and cowardice of an entire nation, Israel would have been completely defeated. If you have a deep desire in your heart to do more with your life than follow the crowd and go after pleasure and prosperity, be part of the Davids of our time! If you feel deep inside a need to make a difference, take a stand like David did. There are not many like him, but they are out there somewhere!

The question to the church is, Do we believe in our God? The time will come and is very near when God will gather the remnants and call out the Davids and all who will join to overcome Islam, the Goliath of our time. The politicians and governments, like King Saul, are too scared to step out and act. They have too much to lose. They want to be elected and need your vote, so they promise what you want to hear. They would rather sacrifice the nation than step out and risk their lives to save our freedom! The government will not be able to stop Islam.

I am well aware that even those people, groups, and organizations that are fighting against Islam and its plans to enforce its law on the Western world strongly avoid being associated with us. We are too radical for them. Jesus was so radical in His preaching and living that the religious leaders were angry at Him all the time. Finally, they killed Him. Jesus' apostles followed Him in the same radical way, and almost all of them were killed for it.

We have to ask ourselves one question: If we never cause trouble because of what we believe, do we really follow Jesus? Jesus caused trouble everywhere He went. At the same time, He ministered to the needy. Here is where the church has lost it. The church is hiding behind its walls having programs and prophetic conferences, prophesying things that may all be true. But instead of acting according to the Word of God, it is going to sleep to escape the danger around us.

## The Church Must Take Responsibility

Islam is of the devil. You cannot sit down with the devil and expect him to work out a fair solution for the conflict he is causing. The devil came to steal, destroy, and kill! A burglar will not ask you for permission to rob your house. A killer will not discuss with you the best way for you to be killed. Let's not be foolish! The devil is evil, and so is Islam.

> He who does what is sinful is of the devil, because the devil has been sinning from the beginning. The reason the Son of God appeared was to destroy the devil's work.
> —1 JOHN 3:8

And in John 10:9–11 Jesus said:

> I am the gate; whoever enters through me will be saved. He will come in and go out, and find pasture. The thief comes only to steal and kill and destroy; I have come that they may have life, and have it to the full. I am the good shepherd. The good shepherd lays down his life for the sheep.

The more we go east, the less Christianity we find in the nations and the less blessed they seem to be materially. The main religions of Asia, much of Africa, and the Middle East are Islam, Hinduism, and Buddhism. People are poor in those countries. Going west to Europe, which was for a long time called in German the *Christliches Abendland*, the Christian Occident, we find a continent that closed the door on God and might become Islamic in the future. It will have to deal with the consequences, and poverty will only be one of them.

The United States of America is still a free nation. For centuries it was known as a Christian nation, the strongest and wealthiest one in the world, but President Obama said we (the U.S.) do not consider ourselves a Christian nation. I personally disagree with his statement. For me it is an alarming sign that America's leadership turns away from Christianity and from the Christian roots of our forefathers. We, like Europe has already done, are closing the door on God. It is still open, but if we wait too long, the government will resist God. With that action, God will give us into the hand of our enemy, Islam!

Abraham had two children. Isaac was the promised son, whose offspring through Jacob were the children of Israel, the family through which Jesus

Christ came. Ishmael was the consequence of Abraham's mistrust toward God, and his offspring fought against Israel from the beginning of their relationship. Islam's roots are traced through the offspring of Abraham's son, Ishmael. We are still fighting the same enemy as our forefathers! We have not shown that we have learned the principles of the Bible—to humble ourselves under God and His Word so that He will establish through us, the church, the body of Christ, His kingdom here on Earth like it is in heaven.

The church does not believe in the truth of humbling ourselves so God can bless us and build His kingdom through us as it is in heaven. The church has forgotten that God gives grace to those who humble themselves, but He rejects the proud (Prov. 3:34; James 4:6; 1 Pet. 5:5).

Government leaders, politicians, and intellectuals try to meet, discuss, and work out arrangements to establish peace agreements. However, these things do not work at all, and there is no peace in this world. Peace will never be created by talking and by political correctness, which is the weakness of the Western world. Islam is taking complete advantage of this weakness. As we try to solve problems by being nice, full of humanism and open to any kind of discussion, Islam is taking us by the hand and leading us to the shambles.

The God of the Bible is the Creator of the universe. He created mankind the way the Bible tells us. He created the Earth! Unless we humble ourselves before Him, repent, and obey His Word there is no hope at all for anyone! This is why the church is called to stand up! The church is the only hope for mankind. The church must realize this and take responsibility for it.

# The COST of FREEDOM

FREEDOM IS NOT FREE. It never was and it never will be! If you really want to fight for it, it will cost you everything, starting with the loss of prestige, acceptance in society, maybe possessions and money, and last but not least the loss of relationships. People can get sick or even die along the way, and marriage or family relationships can suffer or even break!

Job is the perfect example of someone other than Jesus Himself who was willing to pay the whole, entire price to remain loyal to God under all circumstances. He would not let go of God and the truth, and he held on to it in a very, very radical way. Job lost everything; I mean, everything—really! He paid a very high price for the freedom he had in God. Memories of the hurt and pain he suffered would linger in some form in his life, for time alone cannot heal wounds; only the healing hand of the Lord can. But in the end, though, God blessed him abundantly in every area of life!

Because we want to avoid losing things that are precious and dear to us, our freedom is in danger. Not only is our freedom in God in danger, but so are the freedoms we enjoy here in America. We as Christians must stand up against Islam, which is trying to destroy our freedom. As terrible as Islam and its practices are, to a certain extent, its followers are obeying their god more than we are. We have disobeyed one vital, very important scripture:

> I know your deeds, that you are neither cold nor hot. I wish you were either one or the other! So, because you are lukewarm—neither hot nor cold—I am about to spit you out of my mouth.
> —REVELATION 3:15–16

In this verse, Jesus told the church in Laodicea, "I know your deeds." When we look at the Muslims, we see that they are doing deeds. They are out there campaigning, preaching, evangelizing, moving. Are we doing any deeds, except for possibly showing up on Sundays? Are we actually involved in what the church is doing? Are we reaching our society?

Jesus continued His message to the Laodicean church by stating that their deeds were "neither hot nor cold." The deeds of Islam are very wrong;

compared to biblical truth, they are cold! But at least they are doing something. How about our deeds? We are neither hot nor cold, but we have become the church of the middle of the road. We have become what the Bible says God hates, what God spits out of His mouth. We have become the lukewarm church. Jesus basically said, "I wish that you were cold or hot, so because you are lukewarm, I will spit you out of my mouth."

This is the church of today. This is where we are. We are being spat out of God's mouth because we are in the middle of the road. We have tried to please everybody. We have forsaken the Bible, and we have become a lukewarm, pseudo Christian organization filled with political correctness.

How could this happen? Confessing your faith in Christ if you live in Islamic nations will cost your life! However, Christians here in the United States have never really had to pay any price for their faith. Being a Christian is easy in America because we do not have the same level of persecution here as what Christians in other nations face. American Christians have started to take this privilege, this freedom, for granted. They have stopped appreciating the right of free speech and the right to come together each day of the week to praise and worship God without being in harm's way.

The kingdom of God is not a priority for us anymore. With our mouth we proclaim our faith in God and our love for Him, declaring that He is in first place in our lives. Then we go to the service on Sunday and otherwise pursue our own business, which is not much related to a scriptural lifestyle anymore. Christians have become nice and friendly—and selfish. But if you speak truth that challenges their way of living, the friendliest, most loving and kind Christians can suddenly become really angry with you. All their sweet talk about "God is love" is floating only on the surface. They don't really live with or for God. As soon as you ask for a sacrifice, all their sweet talk stops, and they go running off.

Another way we see this is that even if we preach the right things, people have become so numb to the truth that it hardly touches them. When I got saved, smoking cigarettes was not an option for a Christian. Today, however, people can listen to preaching that challenges them to quit smoking and then walk out of the service and light up a cigarette as if it were never mentioned.

Our youth are growing up in this lukewarm environment, and they have learned from the church to go after only their desires, still believing that they are being covered with the blessings of God. They have a worldly lifestyle with immoral relationships and sex, drinking, and partying; and this is sometimes considered OK and accepted by members of the church. When children decide to judge their parents, especially when those parents are serving God, they become displeasing to God. Sadly, parents and sometimes even pastors encourage an ungodly lifestyle for their children. Such people have no fear of God, and they deny the fact that they are sending their children straight to hell. We learn a lesson about this from the story of Eli and his sons.

## The Lesson of Eli and His Sons

The Bible tells us how the spiritual leadership of Israel was very lukewarm in its relationship with God when Eli was serving as a priest at Shiloh. God used him to raise and train Samuel, who became a great prophet, but his own children went astray.

> Now the sons of Eli were worthless men; they did not know the LORD and the custom of the priests with the people. When any man was offering a sacrifice, the priest's servant would come while the meat was boiling, with a three-pronged fork in his hand. Then he would thrust it into the pan, or kettle, or caldron, or pot; all that the fork brought up the priest would take for himself. Thus they did in Shiloh to all the Israelites who came there. Also, before they burned the fat, the priest's servant would come and say to the man who was sacrificing, "Give the priest meat for roasting, as he will not take boiled meat from you, only raw." If the man said to him, "They must surely burn the fat first, and then take as much as you desire," then he would say, "No, but you shall give it to me now; and if not, I will take it by force." Thus the sin of the young men was very great before the LORD, for the men despised the offering of the LORD.
>
> —1 SAMUEL 2:12–17, NAS

We must hold our families to the same standard as others. Showing them favoritism or lowering the standards for their actions is sin in the eyes of the Lord, and it requires repentance! If we do not honor the Lord with our families, our children have the ability to destroy the work of the Lord. They may live and grow up in church, but they may not appreciate the sacrifices and the service of the parents.

In 1 Samuel 2, Eli confronted his sons about the evil they were doing.

> Now Eli was very old; and he heard all that his sons were doing to all Israel, and how they lay with the women who served at the doorway of the tent of meeting. He said to them, "Why do you do such things, the evil things that I hear from all these people? "No, my sons; for the report is not good which I hear the LORD's people circulating. "If one man sins against another, God will mediate for him; but if a man sins against the

Lord, who can intercede for him?" But they would not listen to the voice of their father, for the Lord desired to put them to death.

—1 Samuel 2:22–25, nas

Eli must have missed his chances to discipline his sons. Finally, he had no influence whatsoever. If we as parents wait too long to discipline our children, it is usually too late.

God is not a fool, and He cannot be mocked! He sees right into our hearts.

> Don't be misled: No one makes a fool of God. What a person plants, he will harvest. The person who plants selfishness, ignoring the needs of others—ignoring God!—harvests a crop of weeds. All he'll have to show for his life is weeds! But the one who plants in response to God, letting God's Spirit do the growth work in him, harvests a crop of real life, eternal life.
>
> —Galatians 6:7–8, The Message

God rebuked Eli for his failure and his sin in a serious way!

> Then a man of God came to Eli and said to him, "Thus says the Lord, 'Did I not indeed reveal Myself to the house of your father when they were in Egypt in bondage to Pharaoh's house? Did I not choose them from all the tribes of Israel to be My priests, to go up to My altar, to burn incense, to carry an ephod before Me; and did I not give to the house of your father all the fire offerings of the sons of Israel? Why do you kick at My sacrifice and at My offering which I have commanded in My dwelling, and honor your sons above Me, by making yourselves fat with the choicest of every offering of My people Israel?' Therefore the Lord God of Israel declares, 'I did indeed say that your house and the house of your father should walk before Me forever'; but now the Lord declares, 'Far be it from Me—for those who honor Me I will honor, and those who despise Me will be lightly esteemed. Behold, the days are coming when I will break your strength and the strength of your father's house so that there will not be an old man in your house. You will see the distress of My dwelling, in spite of all the good that I do for Israel; and an old man will not be in your house forever. Yet I will not cut off every man of yours from My altar so that your eyes will fail from weeping and your soul grieve, and all the increase of your house will die in the prime of life. This will be the sign to you which will come concerning your two sons, Hophni and Phinehas: on the same day both of them will die.'"
>
> —1 Samuel 2:27–34, nas

If we let our children go wild because we have become lukewarm and put our families over God and His kingdom, God will not take it lightly. It can cost us the call of God on our lives and can cause many people to suffer. If we don't want our children to "suffer" under a life-giving discipline that leads to repentance, it means that we would rather let them suffer under the curse of selfishness and, if there is no repentance, end up in hell.

## Covenant Relationships

The friendship between David and Jonathan is a great example of the price we may have to pay to fulfill God's plan and vision and help build the kingdom of God. Jonathan, the son of the king, had it made. He was cool and rich and had everything. He did not need to work. He also had many friends and was loved and accepted by everyone. His father was the king, and he would become king one day. That was his future. Then there was David, who had just killed the giant Goliath and had become a hero. He had come out of nowhere, and he had no friends and no education. But he was kind of cool as well.

When Jonathan saw David, he recognized something very important! Deep down in his heart he felt that David was the chosen one. He knew in his heart that he had to make a covenant with David, because he could see that this is what God had planned, and he wanted to be a part of what God was doing. Although Jonathan had the birthright for the kingship, David had been chosen by God. Jonathan knew that he had to give up his right to be king of Israel to fulfill God's plan. Driven by this revelation, he gave David his robe, his tunic, and his sword as a sign of this covenant. What an emotional and anointed moment it must have been!

> After David had finished talking with Saul, Jonathan became one in spirit with David, and he loved him as himself. From that day Saul kept David with him and did not let him return to his father's house. And Jonathan made a covenant with David because he loved him as himself. Jonathan took off the robe he was wearing and gave it to David, along with his tunic, and even his sword, his bow and his belt.
> —1 Samuel 18:1–4

We long for the "alive" feeling of these emotional moments, and living on emotional highs is very characteristic of our times. We are no longer interested in paying the price or sacrificing the things that are important to us but not so important to God! God gives us emotional moments because it makes it easier for us to say yes to Him. Later, though, we have to stick to our word and keep the promise we made in our covenant with Him.

For example, saying, "I do," when we get married is the easy part. In that moment, all is perfect and beautiful, and feelings of love are everywhere.

However, endurance through hard times in life is hard! This is why people run away so easily from covenants and break relationships and betray one another. When the emotions of love are gone, the price to endure and hold on to the covenant gets higher! When it comes to the church, the kingdom of God, many Christians today demonstrate that the price is too high for them to pay.

Jonathan received a revelation from God and said yes to it with obedience that honored God. He unconditionally decided to make a covenant with David without receiving proof or confirmation that David would really be worth it. In fact, Jonathan did not live long enough to see if David really would be the chosen one. Jonathan made his decision based only on his trust in God.

The covenant David and Jonathan made was not of a homosexual nature. Theirs was a love that goes beyond emotions or sex. It was the kind of love God has for us. He proved it to us when He gave His only Son as a sacrifice to save the world from eternal death. This love cannot be touched by any creature, nor can it be understood by the devil, because he is selfish through and through. Never underestimate the power of a true sacrifice!

After a time, Jonathan had to stand up for what was right when his father wanted to kill David out of jealousy. With a sacrificial willingness to lose his relationship with his father, the king, and to even lose his very life, Jonathan asked Saul why he would kill David, an innocent man, for no reason.

> Saul told his son Jonathan and all the attendants to kill David. But Jonathan was very fond of David and warned him, "My father Saul is looking for a chance to kill you. Be on your guard tomorrow morning; go into hiding and stay there. I will go out and stand with my father in the field where you are. I'll speak to him about you and will tell you what I find out." Jonathan spoke well of David to Saul his father and said to him, "Let not the king do wrong to his servant David; he has not wronged you, and what he has done has benefited you greatly. He took his life in his hands when he killed the Philistine. The LORD won a great victory for all Israel, and you saw it and were glad. Why then would you do wrong to an innocent man like David by killing him for no reason?" Saul listened to Jonathan and took this oath: "As surely as the LORD lives, David will not be put to death." So Jonathan called David and told him the whole conversation. He brought him to Saul, and David was with Saul as before.
>
> —1 SAMUEL 19:1–7

Jealousy, which is usually the root of betrayal, attracts evil spirits that painfully torture a person if there is no true repentance. Because of such jealousy,

Saul was very unstable in his emotional life, and he did not keep his promise to Jonathan.

> But an evil spirit from the LORD came upon Saul as he was sitting in his house with his spear in his hand. While David was playing the harp, Saul tried to pin him to the wall with his spear, but David eluded him as Saul drove the spear into the wall. That night David made good his escape.
> —1 SAMUEL 19:9–10

Just two days before Jonathan and David saw each other for the last time, Jonathan confirmed his covenant with David and pledged to learn if his father felt favorably toward David. He willingly, sacrificially released his life, his future, and his inheritance to help David and fulfill the plan of God.

> Then Jonathan said to David: "By the LORD, the God of Israel, I will surely sound out my father by this time the day after tomorrow! If he is favorably disposed toward you, will I not send you word and let you know? But if my father is inclined to harm you, may the LORD deal with me, be it ever so severely, if I do not let you know and send you away safely. May the LORD be with you as he has been with my father. But show me unfailing kindness like that of the LORD as long as I live, so that I may not be killed, and do not ever cut off your kindness from my family—not even when the LORD has cut off every one of David's enemies from the face of the earth." So Jonathan made a covenant with the house of David, saying, "May the LORD call David's enemies to account." And Jonathan had David reaffirm his oath out of love for him, because he loved him as he loved himself.
> —1 SAMUEL 20:12–17

Later, Jonathan died in battle. He was never greatly rewarded on Earth for his tremendous sacrifice, but I believe that when we are in heaven, we will see that he was indeed great before the Lord. He was willing to sacrifice everything and pay the price to stand up against evil and speak the truth so that God's plan and vision might be fulfilled.

## The Pilgrims

We who live in the United States today must consider what freedom will cost us. What will we have to sacrifice in our stand for truth and against Islam? As we in the church do this, I believe we can find great encouragement in the story of the Pilgrims, who established the Plymouth Colony in what would become known as Plymouth, Massachusetts, in 1620.

# The Cost of Freedom

Pilgrims (US), or Pilgrim Fathers (UK), is a name commonly applied to early settlers of the Plymouth Colony in present-day Plymouth, Massachusetts, United States. Their leadership came from a religious congregation of Puritans who had fled a volatile political environment in the East Midlands of England for the relative calm and tolerance of Holland in the Netherlands. Concerned with losing their cultural identity, the group later arranged with English investors to establish a new colony in North America. The colony, established in 1620, became the oldest continuously inhabited British settlement and the second successful English settlement (after the founding of Jamestown, Virginia in 1607) in what was to become the United States of America. The Pilgrims' story of seeking religious freedom has become a central theme of the history and culture of the United States.

The core of the group that would come to be known as the Pilgrims were brought together by a common belief in the ideas promoted by Richard Clyfton, parson at All Saints' Parish Church in Babworth, Nottinghamshire, between 1586 and 1605. This congregation held Separatist beliefs comparable to nonconforming movements (i.e., groups not in communion with the Church of England) led by Henry Barrowe, John Greenwood and Robert Browne. Unlike conforming Puritan groups who maintained their membership in and allegiance to the Church of England, Separatists held that their differences with the Church of England were irreconcilable and that their worship should be organized independently of the trappings, traditions and organization of a central church. William Brewster, a former diplomatic assistant to the Netherlands, was living in the Scrooby manor house, serving as postmaster for the village and bailiff to the Archbishop of York. Having been favorably impressed by Clyfton's services, he had begun participating in Separatist services led by John Smyth in Gainsborough, Lincolnshire. The Separatists had long been controversial. Under the 1559 Act of Uniformity, it was illegal not to attend official Church of England services, with a fine of 12d (£0.05; 2005 equivalent: about £5) for each missed Sunday and holy day. The penalties for conducting unofficial services included imprisonment and larger fines. Under the policy of this time, Barrowe and Greenwood were executed for sedition in 1593....

Scrooby member William Bradford, of Austerfield, kept a journal of the congregation's events that would later be published as *Of Plymouth Plantation*. Of this time, he wrote:

But after these things they could not long continue in any peaceable condition, but were hunted & persecuted on every side, so as their former afflictions were but as flea-bitings in comparison of these which now came upon them. For some were taken & clapt up in prison, others had their houses besett & watcht night and day, & hardly escaped their hands; and ye most were faine to flie & leave their howses & habitations, and the means of their livelehood.

*Decision to leave*

By 1617, although the congregation was stable and relatively secure, there were ongoing issues that needed to be resolved.

Bradford noted that the congregation was aging, compounding the difficulties some had in supporting themselves. Some, having spent through their savings, gave up and returned to England. It was feared that more would follow and that the congregation would become unsustainable. The employment issues made it unattractive for others to come to Leiden, and younger members had begun leaving to find employment and adventure elsewhere. Also compelling was the possibility of missionary work, an opportunity that rarely arose in a Protestant stronghold.

Reasons for departure are suggested by Bradford, when he notes the "discouragements" of the hard life they had in the Netherlands, and the hope of attracting others by finding "a better, and easier place of living"; the "children" of the group being "drawn away by evil examples into extravagance and dangerous courses"; the "great hope, for the propagating and advancing the gospell of the kingdom of Christ in those remote parts of the world."

Edward Winslow's list was similar. In addition to the economic worries and missionary possibilities, he stressed that it was important for the people to retain their English identity, culture and language. They also believed that the English Church in Leiden could do little to benefit the larger community there.

At the same time, there were many uncertainties about moving to such a place as America. Stories had come back from there about failed colonies. There were fears that the native people would be violent, that there would be no source of food or water, that exposure to unknown diseases was possible, and that travel by sea was always hazardous. Balancing all this was a local political situation that was in danger of becoming unstable: the truce in what would be known as the Eighty Years' War was faltering, and there was fear over what the attitudes of Spain toward them might be.

Candidate destinations included Guiana, where the Dutch had already established Essequibo, or somewhere near the existing Virginia settlements. Virginia was an attractive destination because the presence of the older colony might offer better security and trade opportunities. It was thought, however, that they should not settle too near since that might too closely duplicate the political environment back in England. The London Company administered a region of considerable size in the region. The intended settlement location was at the mouth of the Hudson River. This made it possible to settle at a distance that allayed concerns of social conflict, but still provided the military and economic benefits of relative closeness to an established colony.

## Preparations

Not all of the congregation would be able to depart on the first trip. Many members would not be able to settle their affairs within the time constraints, and the budget for travel and supplies was limited. It was decided that the initial settlement should be undertaken primarily by younger and stronger members. The remainder agreed to follow if and when they could.

Robinson would remain in Leiden with the larger portion of the congregation, and Brewster was to lead the American congregation. While the church in America would be run independently, it was agreed that membership would automatically be granted in either congregation to members who moved between the continents.

With personal and business matters agreed upon, supplies and a small ship were procured. *Speedwell* was to bring some passengers from the Netherlands to England, then on to America where it would be kept for the fishing business, with a crew hired for support services during the first year. A second, larger, ship, *Mayflower*, was leased for transport and exploration services.

## Atlantic crossing

Of the 121 combined passengers, 102 were chosen to travel on *Mayflower* with the supplies consolidated. Of these, about half had come by way of Leiden, and about 28 of the adults were members of the congregation. The reduced party finally sailed successfully on September 6/September 16, 1620.

Initially the trip went smoothly, but under way they were met with strong winds and storms. One of these caused a main beam to crack, and although they were more than half the way to their destination, the possibility of turning back was considered. Using a "great iron screw" (probably a piece of house construction equipment) brought along by the colonists, they repaired the ship sufficiently to continue. One passenger, John Howland, was washed overboard in the storm but caught a rope and was rescued.

One crew member and one passenger died before they reached land. A child was born at sea and named "Oceanus".

*Arrival in America*

Land was sighted on November 10/November 20, 1620. It was confirmed that the area was Cape Cod, within the New England territory recommended by Weston. An attempt was made to sail the ship around the cape towards the Hudson River, also within the New England grant area, but they encountered shoals and difficult currents around Malabar (a land mass that formerly existed in the vicinity of present-day Monomoy). It was decided to turn around, and by November 11/November 21 the ship was anchored in what is today known as Provincetown Harbor.

*First landings*

Thorough exploration of the area was delayed for over two weeks because the shallop or pinnace (a smaller sailing vessel) they brought had been partially dismantled to fit aboard the *Mayflower* and was further damaged in transit. Small parties, however, waded to the beach to fetch firewood and attend to long-deferred personal hygiene.

While awaiting the shallop, exploratory parties led by Myles Standish—an English soldier the colonists had met while in Leiden—and Christopher Jones were undertaken. They encountered several old buildings, both European-built and Native-built, and a few recently cultivated fields.

An artificial mound was found near the dunes, which they partially uncovered and found to be a Native grave. Further along, a similar mound, more recently made, was found, and as the colonists feared they might otherwise starve, they ventured to remove some of the provisions which had been placed in the grave. Baskets of maize were found inside, some of which the colonists took and placed into an iron kettle they also found nearby, while they reburied the rest, intending to use the borrowed corn as seed for planting.

William Bradford later recorded in his book, "Of Plymouth Plantation", that after the shallop had been repaired,

"They also found two of the Indian's houses covered with mats, and some of their implements in them; but the people had run away and could not be seen. They also found more corn, and beans of various colours. These they brought away, intending to give them full satisfaction (repayment) when they should meet with any of them,—as about six months afterwards they did.

"And it is to be noted as a special providence of God, and a great mercy to this poor people, that they thus got seed to plant corn the next year, or they might have starved; for they had none, nor any likelihood of getting any, till too late for the planting season."

By December, most of the passengers and crew had become ill, coughing violently. Many were also suffering from the effects of scurvy.

There had already been ice and snowfall, hampering exploration efforts. During the first winter, 47% of them died.

## *Contact*

Explorations resumed on December 6/December 16. The shallop party—seven colonists from Leiden, three from London, and seven crew—headed south along the cape and chose to land at the area inhabited by the Nauset people (roughly, present-day Brewster, Chatham, Eastham, Harwich and Orleans), where they saw some native people on the shore, who ran when the colonists approached. Inland they found more mounds, one containing acorns, which they exhumed and left, and more graves, which they decided not to dig.

Remaining ashore overnight, they heard cries near the encampment. The following morning, they were met by native people who proceeded to shoot at them with arrows. The colonists retrieved their firearms and shot back, then chased the native people into the woods but did not find them. There was no more contact with native people for several months.

## *Settlement*

Continuing westward, the shallop's mast and rudder were broken by storms, and their sail was lost. Rowing for safety, they encountered the harbor formed by the current Duxbury and Plymouth barrier beaches and stumbled on land in the darkness. They remained at this spot—Clark's Island—for two days to recuperate and repair equipment.

Resuming exploration on Monday, December 11/December 21, 1620, the party crossed over to the mainland and surveyed the area that ultimately became the settlement. The anniversary of this survey is observed in Massachusetts as Forefathers' Day and is traditionally associated with the Plymouth Rock landing legend. This land was especially suited to winter building because the land had already been cleared, and the tall hills provided a good defensive position.

The cleared village, known as Patuxet to the Wampanoag people, was abandoned about three years earlier following a plague that killed all of its residents. Because the disease involved hemorrhaging, the "Indian fever" is assumed to have been fulminating smallpox introduced by European traders. The outbreak had been severe enough that the colonists discovered unburied skeletons in abandoned dwellings. With the local population in such a weakened state, the colonists faced no resistance to settling there.

The exploratory party returned to *Mayflower*, which was then brought to the harbor on December 16/December 26. Only nearby sites were evaluated, with a hill in Plymouth (so named on earlier charts) chosen on December 19/December 29.

Construction commenced immediately, with the first common house nearly completed by January 9/January 19. At this point, single men were ordered to join with families. Each extended family was assigned a plot and built its own dwelling. Supplies were brought ashore, and the settlement was mostly complete by early February.

Between the landing and March, only 47 colonists had survived the diseases they contracted on the ship. During the worst of the sickness, only six or seven of the group were able and willing to feed and care for the rest. In this time, half the *Mayflower* crew also died.

William Bradford became governor in 1621 upon the death of John Carver, served for eleven consecutive years, and was elected to various other terms until his death in 1657. The patent of Plymouth Colony was surrendered by Bradford to the freemen in 1640, minus a small reserve of three tracts of land. On March 22, 1621, the Pilgrims of Plymouth Colony signed a peace treaty with Massasoit of the Wampanoags.

The colony contained roughly what is now Bristol County, Plymouth County, and Barnstable County, Massachusetts.

When the Massachusetts Bay Colony was reorganized and issued a new charter as the Province of Massachusetts Bay in 1691, Plymouth ended its history as a separate colony.[1]

The General Society of Mayflower Descendants (also known as the Mayflower Society) is a hereditary organization of individuals who have documented their descent from one or more of the 102 passengers who arrived on the *Mayflower* in 1620 at what is now Plymouth, Massachusetts. The Society was founded at Plymouth in 1897.[2]

Thanksgiving or Thanksgiving Day, currently celebrated on the fourth Thursday in November, has been an annual tradition in the United States since 1863. Thanksgiving was historically a religious observation to give thanks to God.

The first Thanksgiving was celebrated to give thanks to God for helping the Pilgrims of Plymouth Colony survive the brutal winter. The first Thanksgiving feast lasted three days providing enough food for 53 pilgrims and 90 Native Americans. The feast consisted of fowl, venison, fish, lobster, clams, berries, fruit, pumpkin,and squash. William Bradford's note that, "besides waterfowl, there was great store of wild turkeys, of which they took many," probably gave rise to the American tradition of turkey at Thanksgiving.

## *1619 Thanksgiving, the Virginia Colony*

On December 4, 1619, 38 English settlers arrived at Berkeley Hundred, which comprised about 8,000 acres (32 km$^2$) on the north bank of the James River, near Herring Creek, in an area then known as Charles Cittie, about 20 miles (32 km) upstream from Jamestown, where the first permanent settlement of the Colony of Virginia had been established on May 14, 1607.

The group's charter required that the day of arrival be observed yearly as a "day of thanksgiving" to God. On that first day, Captain John Woodleaf held the service of thanksgiving. As quoted from the section of the Charter of Berkeley Hundred specifying the thanksgiving service: "We ordaine that the day of our ships arrival at the place assigned for plantacon in the land of Virginia shall be yearly and perpetually kept holy as a day of thanksgiving to Almighty God."

## *1621 Thanksgiving, the Pilgrims at Plymouth*

The modern Thanksgiving holiday traces its origins from a 1621 celebration at the Plymouth Plantation, where the Plymouth settlers held a harvest feast after a successful growing season. It is this iconic event that is generally referred to as the "First Thanksgiving."

Squanto, a Patuxet Native American who resided with the Wampanoag tribe, taught the Pilgrims how to catch eel and grow corn and served as an interpreter for them (Squanto had learned English while enslaved in Europe and during travels in England). Additionally the Wampanoag leader Massasoit had caused food stores to be donated to the fledgling colony during the first winter when supplies brought from England were insufficient. The Pilgrims set apart a day to celebrate at Plymouth immediately after their first harvest, in 1621. At the time, this was not regarded as a Thanksgiving observance; harvest festivals existed in English and Wampanoag tradition alike. Several colonists gave personal accounts of the 1621 feast in Plymouth, Massachusetts. The Pilgrims, most of whom were Separatists, are not to be confused with Puritans who established their own Massachusetts Bay Colony nearby (current day Boston) in 1628 and had very different religious beliefs.

William Bradford, in *Of Plymouth Plantation:*

Thus they found the Lord to be with them in all their ways, and to bless their outgoings and incomings, for which let His holy name have the praise forever, to all posterity. They began now to gather in the small harvest they had, and to fit up their houses and dwellings against winter, being all well recovered in health and strength and had all things in good plenty. For as some were thus employed in affairs abroad, others were exercised in fishing, about cod and bass and other fish, of which they took good store, of which every family had their portion. All the summer there was no want; and now began to come in store of fowl, as winter approached, of which this place did abound when they came first (but afterward decreased by degrees). And besides waterfowl there was great store of wild turkeys, of which they took many, besides venison, etc. Besides, they had about a peck a meal a week to a person, or now since harvest, Indian corn to the proportion. Which made many afterwards write so largely of their plenty here to their friends in England, which were not feigned but true reports.

Edward Winslow, in *Mourt's Relation*:

Our harvest being gotten in, our governor sent four men on fowling, that so we might after a special manner rejoice together after we had gathered the fruits of our labor. They four in one day killed as much fowl as, with a little help beside, served the company almost a week. At which time, amongst other recreations, we exercised our arms, many of the Indians coming amongst us, and among the rest their greatest king Massasoit, with some ninety men, whom for three days we entertained and feasted, and they went out and killed five deer, which we brought to the plantation and bestowed on our governor, and upon the captain and others. And although it be not always so plentiful as it was at this time with us, yet by the goodness of God, we are so far from want that we often wish you partakers of our plenty.[3]

## There Is Hope for Us

There is hope for us when we trust in Jesus Christ, the Son of God, the only way to the God our Pilgrim forefathers worshiped. Those bold and brave men were grateful to God, and our nation was founded on their spirit of gratefulness. Many Americans have lost this spirit, but if we repent, there is hope that we can regain it. We cannot allow the force called Islam to destroy everything the Pilgrims lived and died for. We cannot give up and, with no resistance, let go of what God has given us! We must fight with all our strength and life for the church to be the way God wants it to be.

Our schools and government officials still have the tradition of reciting our Pledge of Allegiance.

> The Pledge of Allegiance of the United States is an oath of loyalty to the national flag and the republic of the United States of America, originally composed by Francis Bellamy in 1892. The Pledge has been modified

four times since then, with the most recent change adding the words "under God" in 1954. The Pledge is predominantly sworn by children in public schools in response to state laws requiring the Pledge to be offered. Congressional sessions open with the swearing of the Pledge, as do government meetings at local levels, meetings held by the Royal Rangers, Boy Scouts of America, the Freemasons and their concordant bodies, other organizations, and some sporting events.

The current version of the Pledge of Allegiance reads:

I pledge allegiance to the flag of the United States of America, and to the republic for which it stands, one nation under God, indivisible, with liberty and justice for all.

According to the United States Flag Code, the Pledge "should be rendered by standing at attention facing the flag with the right hand over the heart. When not in uniform men should remove any non-religious headdress with their right hand and hold it at the left shoulder, the hand being over the heart. Persons in uniform should remain silent, face the flag, and render the military salute."[4]

If we pledge our loyalty to a nation, how much more we should offer it to the church, the body of Jesus Christ, the Son of God? The challenge before us as Christians is that we must unite. We must not remain lukewarm, but instead we must become hot and be radical for Christ. Let us stand up for the truth and protest together against Islam. Let us organize and make our voices heard. As those who belong to the family of God through faith in Christ, let us honor His sacrifice! Let us do the right thing and build the overcoming church, which God is calling us to be.

# Appendix A
# The CONTRAST BETWEEN JESUS CHRIST and MOHAMMED

THE CENTRAL FIGURE OF CHRISTIANITY is Jesus Christ; the central figure of Islam, Mohammed. In the search for truth then, it is only reasonable to compare these two men in order to see who is from God, and who is from the devil.

### Births
Jesus was born miraculously to a virgin, conceived by the Holy Spirit. There was nothing miraculous about Mohammed's birth.

### Prophecy
The birth, life, and crucifixion of Jesus were prophesied in well over one hundred places in the Old Testament with remarkable accuracy. The combined weight of these prophesies alone is enough to prove beyond any reasonable doubt that Jesus truly was the Messiah and the Son of God. The coming of Mohammed was not foretold by any prophets. There have been attempts by certain Muslims to claim that the Bible prophesied the coming of Muhammad in John 14, 15, and 16, but these scriptures are clearly defined as prophesying the coming of the Holy Spirit, who has come and remains with us today.

### Miracles
Jesus performed many miracles; He even commanded His disciples to "heal the sick, raise the dead, cleanse those who have leprosy, drive out demons" (Matt. 10:8) which they then did. Jesus is recorded to have performed over thirty miracles, and John writes that "Jesus did many other things as well" (John 21:25). Mohammed did not perform any miracles. The only thing he ever claimed as a miracle was the Quran, which we have seen, and will see further in the remaining appendices, that this was no miracle at all.

### Sin
Jesus lived a perfect life. Mohammed was full of sin, and the Quran itself says that Mohammed was "but a man" (Surah 18:110).

## Forgiveness

When confronted with adultery, Jesus said:

> If any one of you is without sin, let him be the first to throw a stone at her."...Jesus straightened up and asked her, "Woman, where are they? Has no one condemned you?" "No one, sir," she said. "Then neither do I condemn you," Jesus declared. "Go now and leave your life of sin."
> —John 8:7–11

What was Mohammed's reaction?

> Then the Prophet said, "Take him away and stone him to death."[1]

## Deaths

The death of Jesus was anticipated and even ordained by God for a specific purpose: "He is the atoning sacrifice for our sins, and not only for ours but also for the sins of the whole world" (1 John 2:2).

Mohammed's death came without warning, without plan, and without forethought. His death served no purpose and was certainly not an atonement for anyone's sins. The only way to heaven in Islam is to do more good deeds than bad, or to die in Jihad.

## Resurrection

Mohammed, just like Buddha, Confucius, and every other leader of false religions, lies dead and rotting in a grave. Jesus entered the grave, but He did not remain. Jesus is the only one ever to have lived who can say, "I am the Living One; I was dead, and behold I am alive for ever and ever! And I hold the keys of death and Hades" (Rev. 1:18).

## Conclusion

Ultimately Mohammed does not compare to Jesus in any way. His life, his mission, and his death all signify worldly origins. The apostle Paul said it the most clearly when he spoke of Jesus:

> ...who through the Spirit of *holiness was declared with power to be the Son of God* by his resurrection from the dead: Jesus Christ our Lord.
> —Romans 1:4, emphasis added

Nothing was declared of Mohammed with power. His declarations were only backed by his word and by the sword and scimitar, which followed his command to fight in Medina. The spread of Christianity can only be accounted for by the sincere belief, based on eyewitness accounts, in the resurrection of Jesus Christ—possible only if this miracle was, and is, entirely true.

## Appendix B
# MUSLIM CLAIMS ABOUT the QURAN
*False Claims About the Quran*

"MOHAMMAD SAW THE QURAN AS the warrant of his prophethood. Moslem scholars are unanimous in regarding the Quran as Mohammad's miracle."[1]

The Quran is considered by Muslims to be:

1. Delivered in perfect Arabic
2. Placed on a table in heaven
3. Transmitted perfectly from the original
4. Untranslatable
5. Utterly unique literature

**Perfect Arabic?**

The idea that the Quran is written in perfect Arabic comes from several passages in the Quran; namely, Surah 2:177, 192; 3:59; 4:162; 5:69; 7:160; 13:28; 20:66; 63:10. The idea is essentially that Allah wrote it in heaven and then it was "sent down" to Mohammed verbatim. Because Allah wrote it, it must be perfect.

Noldeke, in the *Encyclopedia of Religion*, writes:

> On the whole, while many parts of the Koran undoubtedly have considerable rhetorical power, even over an unbelieving reader, the book aesthetically considered, is by no means a first rate performance....Let us look at some of the more extended narratives. It has already been noticed how vehement and abrupt they are where they ought to be characterized by epic repose. Indispensable links, both in the expression and in the sequence of events, are often omitted, so that to understand these histories is sometimes far easier for us than for those who heard them first, because we know most of them from better sources. Along with this, there is a good deal of superfluous verbiage; and nowhere do we find a steady advance in the narration. Contrast in these respects the history of Joseph and its glaring improprieties with the admirably conceived and admirably

executed story in Genesis. Similar faults are found in the non-narrative portions of the Koran. The connexion of ideas is extremely loose, and even the syntax betrays great awkwardness. Anacolutha [want of syntactical sequence; when the latter part of a sentence does not grammatically fit the earlier] are of frequent occurrence, and cannot be explained as conscious literary devices. Many sentences begin with a "when" or "on the day when" which seems to hover in the air, so that commentators are driven to supply a "think of this" or some such ellipsis. Again, there is no great literary skill evinced in the frequent and needless harping on the same words and phrases; in xviii, for example "till that" occurs no fewer than eight times. Mahomet in short, is not in any sense a master of style.[2]

## Table in heaven?

We have already seen in chapter two many reasons to doubt the idea of the Quran's heavenly origin. The Quran is full of "revelations" meant for Mohammed alone. Beyond this, the very principle of abrogation from Surah 2, verse 104, "Whatever communications We abrogate or cause to be forgotten, We bring one better than it or like it," makes good sense for a dictator who finds it convenient to change laws around, but if Allah wrote this book from the beginning of time, is it really likely that in the span of twenty-three years he would need to change so many of his rulings?

## Transmitted perfectly?

A frequent claim of Muslims is that the text of the Quran is completely free from error or dispute. In talks with Christians, they may claim that the Bible has been corrupted over the years, but the Quran should be believed because the original text still exists.

Naturally, existence of an original text would not prove its correctness, but is this claim even true? Unfortunately for the Muslim who makes these assertions, this is utterly false. Ibn Warraq explains:

> After Muhammad's death in A.D. 632, there was no collection of his revelations. Consequently, many of his followers tried to gather all the known revelations and write them down in codex form. Soon we had the codices of several scholars....As Islam spread, we eventually had what became known as the Metropolitan Codices in the centers of Mecca, Medina, Damascus, Kufa, and Basra. As we saw earlier, Uthman tried to bring order to this chaotic situation by canonizing the Medinan Codex, copies of which were sent to all the metropolitan centers, with orders to destroy all the other codices.

Uthman's codex was supposed to standardize the consonantal text; yet we find that many of the variant traditions of this consonantal text survived well into the fourth Islamic century...After having settled the consonants, Muslims still had to decide what vowels to employ: using different vowels, of course, rendered different readings.[3]

This eventually led to seven different and separate readings of the Quran. Charles Adams said:

It is of some importance to call attention to a possible source of misunderstanding with regard to the variant readings of the Quran. The seven [versions] refer to actual differences in the written and oral text, to distinct versions of the Quranic verses, whose differences, though they may not be great, are nonetheless real and substantial.[4]

## Untranslatable

Another frequent claim about the Quran is that it can only be understood in Arabic, and that anything outside of the Arabic text is untrustworthy. While this may have some merit in a strict sense that there is no direct translation for certain words, it is a simple question of logic to realize that the text is of course translatable. All languages can be translated, and most are translated on a regular basis. Where meanings are not immediately understandable, commentaries and lexicons, critical analysis and textual criticism, resolve this problem easily for the determined scholar of the language and the text.

Furthermore, there are of course many translations of the Quran in existence today. Wikipedia lists forty-five translations into English alone.[5] There have obviously been a great deal of people who seemed to think that this feat was more than worth the attempt.

## Conclusion

The true history of the collection and the creation of the text of the Quran reveals that the Muslim claims are indeed fictitious and not in accord with the facts. The fingerprints of Mohammed can be seen on every page as a witness to its human origin.

# *Appendix C*
# BLATANT ERRORS in the QURAN

In this section we will discuss a variety of problems with the Quran; not theological problems, or problems stemming from the religion, but just plain errors.

## How Many Days of Creation?

Your Guardian-Lord is Allah, Who created the heavens and the earth in six days.
—Surah 7:54

Say: Is it that ye deny Him Who created the earth in two Days?...He set on the (earth), mountains standing firm, high above it, and bestowed blessings on the earth, and measure therein all things to give them nourishment in due proportion, in four Days...So He completed them as seven firmaments in two Days.
—Surah 41:9–10, 12

In the first passage, heaven and earth were created in six days. Add up the days in the second, and it took eight days. Either one account is wrong, or both are wrong, but they most certainly cannot both be right.

## Violations of Time in History

Another testament to the fact that Mohammed had no original sources in front of him is the strange array of people whom he pictured living and working together. Consider just a few of these many situations:

1. Nimrod and Abraham (Surah 21:51–71; 29:16–17; 37:97–98)
2. Haman and Moses (Surah 28:35–42; 40:36–37)
3. Mary and Aaron (Surah 19:27–28 claims that Mary was Aaron's sister!)
4. Moses and the Flood (Surah 7:133)
5. Pharaoh and the Tower of Babel (Surah 40:36–37)

Mohammed makes it sound as if all these people and events lived and occurred at the same time. In truth, with the nature of fireside storytelling, he probably just had no idea.

### Crucifixion by Pharaoh?

> Said Pharaoh: "Believe ye in Him before I give you permission? Surely this is a trick which ye have planned in the city to drive out its people: but soon shall ye know (the consequences). Be sure I will cut off your hands and your feet on apposite sides, and I will cause you all to die on the cross.
> —SURAH 7:123–124

As a simple matter of historical fact, crucifixion did not exist at the time of Moses, but was invented centuries later by the Romans.

### Who Was the First Muslim?

Another big problem in Quran consistency: who was the first Muslim? As we all know, you can only have one "first," but what of Mohammed's list?

1. Mohammed? (Surah 6:14, 163)
2. Moses? (Surah 7:143)
3. Some Egyptians? (Surah 26:51)
4. Abraham? (Surah 2:127–133; 3:67)
5. Adam? (Surah 2:37)

Each one of these clearly states that they were the first to believe or the first to receive revelation from Allah. There can only be one first, so this is a problem.

### What Do People Eat in Hell?

1. Only Dhari? (Surah 88:6)
2. Only foul pus from the washing of wounds? (Surah 69:36)
3. The tree of Zaqqum as well? (Surah 37:66)

In court cases, when a witness gives you three conflicting stories at three different times, you generally throw out all results as untrustworthy. Perhaps Mohammed should have thought out some of the details a little better.

## Adultery

Surah 24, Verse 2 states that:

> The woman and the man guilty of adultery or fornication—flog each of them with a hundred stripes.

Yet in Sahih al-Bukhari, Volume 8, Book 82, Number 806, Mohammed condemned adulterers to stoning.

Furthermore, Surah 4:15–16 says that:

> If any of your women are guilty of lewdness, take the evidence of four (reliable) witnesses from amongst you against them; and if they testify, confine them to houses until death do claim them, or Allah ordain for them some (other) way.

So is the punishment stoning? flogging? or lifelong house arrest? Unfortunately sharia courts throughout the centuries have often settled on harsher of the three.

## The Gospel and Torah

Oh look, it turns out the Jews *do* have the true scripture!

> But how do they come to you for decision while they have the Taurat (Torah), in which *is* the (plain) Decision of Allah; yet even after that, they turn away. For they are not (really) believers.
> —Surah 5:43, Hilali-Khan, emphasis added

And so do the Christians!

> And We caused Jesus, son of Mary, to follow in their footsteps, confirming that which was (revealed) before him in the Torah, and We bestowed on him the Gospel wherein *is* guidance and a light, confirming that which was (revealed) before it in the Torah... *Let the People of the Gospel judge by that which Allah hath revealed therein.* Whoso judgeth not by that which Allah hath revealed: such are evil-livers.
> —Surah 5:46–47, Pikthal, emphasis added

Islamic tradition tells us that Mohammed believed his coming was prophesied in both the Torah and the Gospel. This explains why he would be so confident in telling the Jews and Christians to turn to their own scriptures for confirmation about his prophethood. The trouble was, they did turn to their scriptures and found Mohammed to be a false prophet. It seems once again he was a little too over-confident in his knowledge of scripture.

## A Borrowed Religion

An excellent book for further reading is *The Origins of the Koran*, edited by Ibn Warraq. In it, he puts forth a thorough analysis of the transmission of the Quranic text, and also explains many of the origins of a large range of the stories in the Quran. Consider a few short excerpts:

> The Jews were numerous and powerful throughout Arabia, and Muhammad, having sought their conversion in vain, at last fought against them and banished them from the country. But in the meantime he had taken much of his teaching from their books, the Talmud, their commentaries, etc....Thus there is the story of Cain and Aben, and of their parents weeping while the raven showed how to bury the dead; Abraham cast by Nimrod into the fire unhurt; the Queen of Sheba uncovering her legs as she walked before Solomon over the glass floor, which she takes for a sheet of water; the descent of Harut and Marut and other spirits from above to tempt mankind; Sammael, the Angel of Death, speaking out of the golden calf—and other fictitious takes too numerous to mention...

> There were many Christian tribes in Arabia belonging to heretical sects who had sought refuge there from persecution in Roman lands. Little versed in their own Scriptures, they spent the time in imaginary and childish fables. The Prophet, longing for a universal faith, listened gladly to such stories, which thus became the source of much we find in the Koran.

> First we have the fairy tale of the cave wherein the seven sleepers slumbered for ages, fearing persecution. Next we have endless stories of the Virgin Mary, both in the Koran and with vast detail also in tradition; her mother Hannah, her childhood as fed by angels in the temple, Joseph chosen by a miraculous rod, etc., much as in the Proto-Evangelium and other Egyptian and Coptic writings. Then there are the tales of Jesus, as of his speaking in the cradle, breathing life into birds of clay, etc....such Coptic books as the Gospel of St. Thomas. Thus we have the descent of the Table from Heaven (derived no doubt from the table of the Lord's Super); the promise by Jesus of a prophet to come, called Ahmed....the notion that the resemblance only, and not the real person, of Christ was slain, derived from the heretic Basilides, etc. Passing over much of interest, we may close our review of Christian sources by notice of the *balance*, briefly mentioned in the Koran, but surrounded by a vast variety of Coptic tales. Two Egyptian books (one of ancient date placed in the tombs to be read by the dead) are quoted at length...and strange sights are given of Adam and Abraham in the heavens beyond.

In conclusion, Warraq writes:

> ...sources of Islam...have been altogether human and misleading. They all passed through the Prophet's mind as he composed the Koran, which thus bears throughout the impress of his own heart and character. One good thing there is in it, namely, a thorough testimony of the Gospel and Torah; all true Muslims are accordingly invited to study both, and thus through our Savior Christ obtain the true promises of their father Abraham.[1]

## Lost in Translation?

Mohammed got many, many stories from the Bible mixed up, placed out of context, or just plain confused. But what should we expect? Mohammed was illiterate and lived a long distance from orthodox Christianity and orthodox Judaism. The stories he heard from distant travelers, as a product of their own culture, had also been mixed up with various heretical sources. Mohammed claimed that Islam was a natural continuation of Christianity, so we have two choices: Mohammed was retelling old stories he had heard in his travels with his own special Islamic twist, or everyone else was wrong and he received these corrections straight from God. The magnitude of these errors, along with the insignificance to doctrinal issues, proves beyond a reasonable doubt that Mohammed was just retelling old stories.

## Mistakes About the Trinity

Surah 5:16 of the Quran says:

> And behold! Allah will say: "O Jesus the son of Mary! Didst thou say unto men, worship me and my mother as gods in derogation of Allah?"

This passage quite obviously seems to be a rebuke to the Christians, but there's an obvious problem here. No Christian believes that the Trinity consists of God, Jesus, and Mary! Someone might say, "Well, he was rebuking the Catholics," but of course the Catholic Church also does not think this is the definition of the Trinity.

Mohammed clearly misunderstood this and then decided he needed to rebuke it as polytheism in the Quran. In doing so, he displayed his ignorance of what Christians actually believe for all generations to come.

### The Flood and Noah's Sons

In the Bible, all three of Noah's sons were saved on the ark (Gen. 7:1, 7, 13), but in the Quran (Surah 11:32–48) one of the sons drowned in the flood.

**Joseph**

The Quran says the name of the person who bought Joseph was Aziz, but in the Bible it was Potiphar (Surah 12:2; Gen. 37:6).

**Moses**

In the Quran, Pharaoh's wife adopts Moses (Surah 28:8–9). In the Bible, it is his daughter (Exod. 2:5).

**Praying toward Jerusalem**

The Quran says that Jews pray towards Jerusalem. This may have been a tradition in the time of Mohammed, but has certainly never been an orthodox belief of Judaism.

## Conclusion

It is easy enough for Christians to see that Islam contradicts the Bible. When we see in addition that Mohammed regularly contradicted himself, then a whole new picture comes to light. The Quran can easily be explained through the convergence of seventh-century Arabian cultures. The spread of Islam can be explained by man's lust for women, power, and wealth. Christianity is the only way that offers a real solution—the only religion that is true. The only real explanation of the religion of Mohammed is that Islam is of the devil.

# NOTES

### Introduction
1. Rick Joyner, *The Vision* (Nashville, TN: Thomas Nelson, 2001).

### 1—Taking a Stand for the Truth
1. "Islam," *Wikipedia.com*, http://en.wikipedia.org/wiki/Islam#cite_note-1 (accessed April 6, 2010).
2. Information available online at http://news.bbc.co.uk/2/hi/europe/7842344.stm (accessed April 26, 2010).
3. Information available online at http://www.foxnews.com/story/0,2933,494424,00.html (accessed April 19, 2010).

### 2—The Nature of Islam and Its Beliefs
1. Thomas Jefferson's letter to the Danbury Baptist Association, http://www.loc.gov/loc/lcib/9806/danpre.html (accessed May 26, 2010).
2. Victor Khalil and Deborah Khalil, "When Muslims Meet Christians," *Christian Herald*, July/Aug. 1988, 43.
3. Robert Morey, *The Islamic Invasion* (Eugene, OR: Harvest House Publishers, 1992).
4. Ibid., 40.
5. Ibn Warraq, *Why I Am Not a Muslim* (Amherst, NY: Prometheus Books, 1995), 39.
6. Ibid., 101.
7. James Hastings, ed. *Encyclopedia of Religion and Ethics*, vol. 1 (London: T&T Clark, Publishers, 1926), p. 660
8. M. M. Bravmann, M. M. "The Spiritual Background of Early Islam: Studies in Ancient Arab Concepts," *Journal of the American Oriental Society*, Apr./Jun. 1974, 235–237.
9. Robert Morey, *The Islamic Invasion*.
10. Cyril Glasse, *The Concise Encyclopedia of Islam* (New York: Harper & Row, 1989).
11. Ibid.
12. Robert Morey, *The Islamic Invasion*.
13. Samuel M. Zwemer, *The Moslem Doctrine of God* (Garland, TX: American Tract Society, 190), 5.
14. C. S. Lewis, *Mere Christianity* (New York: HarperCollins, 2001), 40.
15. Samuel M. Zwemer, *The Moslem Doctrine of God*.
16. C. S. Lewis, *The Problem of Pain*, (New York: HarperCollins, 2001), 18.
17. *Sahih al-Bukhari*, Volume 5, Book 58, Number 266
18. Robert Spencer, *The Truth about Muhammad* (Washington, DC: Regnery Press, 2007).
19. *Sahih al-Bukhari*, Volume 9, Book 87, Number 111

20. Samuel Zwemer, *Islam: A Challenge to Faith* (New York: Student Volunteer Movement for Foreign Missions, 1907).

21. Ali Dashti, *Twenty-Three Years*, translated from the Persian by F. R. C. Bagley (London: George Allen & Unwin Ltd., 198).5

22. Alvin Schmidt, *The Great Divide* (Salisbury, MA: Regina Orthodox Press, 2004).

23. Samuel Zwemer, *Islam: A Challenge to Faith*.

24. Eugene Caner, *Unveiling Islam: An Insider's Look at Muslim Life and Beliefs* (Grand Rapids, MI: Kregel Publications, 2009).

25. *Sahih al-Bukhari*, Volume 7, Book 62, Number 64

26. *Sahih al-Bukhari* Volume 5, Book 59, Number 551 and Number 713

27. Jonathan P. Berkey, *The Formation of Islam: Religion and Society in the Near East, 600–1800* (Cambridge, England: Cambridge University Press), 70.

28. Samuel Zwemer, *Islam: A Challenge to Faith*.

### 4—A Masquerade of Peace and Tolerance

1. Robert Spencer, *The Complete Infidel's Guide to the Koran* (Washington, DC: Regnery Press, 2009).

2. Information available online at http://www.youtube.com/watch?v=KtX3mTdJ9Lk&feature=related (accessed April 26, 2010).

3. Information available online at http://www.irfi.org/articles/articles_151_200/triple_talaq.htm (accessed April 26, 2010).

4. Information available online at http://www.youtube.com/watch#!v=SpffWcPD9iA&feature=related (accessed April 26, 2010).

5. Information available online at http://en.wikipedia.org/wiki/Honor_killing (accessed April 26, 2010).

6. Ibid.

7. Information available online at http://en.wikipedia.org/wiki/Honor_killing#As_a_cultural_practice (accessed April 26, 2010).

8. Information available online at http://www.rozanehmagazine.com/julyaugust02/Mayjune02new/wpakistan.html (accessed April 26, 2010).

9. Information available online at http://en.wikipedia.org/wiki/Ghazala_Khan; http://www.telegraph.co.uk/news/worldnews/europe/denmark/1522643/Honour-killing-family-jailed-over-shot-bride.html (accessed April 26, 2010).

10. Information available online at http://articles.latimes.com/2005/may/24/world/fg-turkwomen24 (accessed April 26, 2010).

11. Information available online at http://www.cleveland.com/whateverhappened/index.ssf/2000/07/cousin_acquitted_in_killing.html (accessed April 26, 2010).

12. Information available online at http://www.cnn.com/WORLD/9512/honor_killings (accessed April 26, 2010).

13. Information available online at http://www.shieldofachilles.net/2007/10/because-women-here-have-so-many-rights.html (accessed April 26, 2010).

14. Information available online at http://www.guardian.co.uk/editor/story/0,12900,1053731,00.html (accessed April 26, 2010).

15. Information available online at http://www.cnn.com/WORLD/9512/honor_killings (accessed April 26, 2010).

16. Information available online at http://en.wikipedia.org/wiki/Fadime_Sahindal; http://community.seattletimes.nwsource.com/archive/?date=20020308&slug=honorkill08 (accessed April 26, 2010).

17. Information available online at http://www.riverfronttimes.com/content/printVersion/972718 (accessed April 26, 2010).

18. Information available online at http://www.cbc.ca/canada/montreal/story/2009/07/24/montreal-canal-deaths-rona-mohammed-siblings.html (accessed April 26, 2010).

19. Information available online at http://atlasshrugs2000.typepad.com/atlas_shrugs/2009/03/again-this-is-not-some-third-world-islamic-hellhole-this-is-germany-another-muslim-girl-severely-beaten-repeatedly.html (accessed April 26, 2010).

20. "U.S. TV Network Founder Charged with Beheading Wife," Reuters, February 17, 2009.

21. Information available online at http://www.foxnews.com/story/0,2933,391531,00.html (accessed April 26, 2010).

22. Information available online at http://www.spiegel.de/international/germany/0,1518,555667-2,00.html (accessed April 26, 2010).

23. Information available online at http://www.ekurd.net/mismas/articles/misc2008/4/kurdsworldwide303.htm (accessed April 26, 2010).

24. Information available online at http://www.guardian.co.uk/uk/2007/mar/13/ukcrime (accessed April 26, 2010).

25. Information available online at http://www.cnn.com/2008/WORLD/meast/02/08/iraq.women/index.html (accessed April 26, 2010).

26. Information available online at http://www.timesonline.co.uk/tol/news/uk/article675686.ece (accessed April 26, 2010).

27. Information available online at http://www.indymedia.ie/article/78088 (accessed April 26, 2010).

28. Information available online at http://www.aqsaparvez.com; http://www.thestar.com/news/gta/article/284350 (accessed April 26, 2010).

29. Information available online at http://www.independent.co.uk/news/uk/crime/muslim-husband-who-killed-his-wife-and-children-because-of-their-western-ways-437199.html (accessed April 26, 2010).

30. Information available online at http://www.dailymail.co.uk/news/article-452288/The-moment-teenage-girl-stoned-death-loving-wrong-boy.html (accessed April 26, 2010).

31. Information available online at http://www.haaretz.com/hasen/pages/ShArt.jhtml?itemNo=705184 (accessed April 26, 2010).

32. Information available online at http://www.dailymail.co.uk/news/article-506686/Family-turned-blind-eye-teenage-bride-beaten-death-arranged-husband.html; http://www.yorkshireeveningpost.co.uk/news/Woman-suffered-39worst-injuries-I.1955574.jp (accessed April 26, 2010).

33. John Azumah, *The Legacy of Arab-Islam in Africa* (Oxford: OneWorld Publications, 2001).

34. Ibid.
35. Ibid.
36. Rachel Ehrenfeld, *Funding Evil* (Los Angeles, CA: Bonus Books, 2005).
37. Information available online at https://www.cia.gov/library/publications/the-world-factbook/geos/sa.htm (accessed April 26, 2010).
38. Information available online at http://archive.arabnews.com/?page=1&section=0&article=46670&d=12&m=6&y=2004 (accessed April 26, 2010).
39. Information available online at http://www.alharamainsermons.org/eng/modules.php?name=News&file=article&sid=71; http://news.bbc.co.uk/2/hi/programmes/panorama/4171950.stm; http://www.adl.org/anti_semitism/arab/Arab_Anti-Semitism.pdf (accessed April 26, 2010).
40. Peter Hammond, *Slavery, Terrorism, and Islam: The Historical Roots and Contemporary Threat* (San Jose, CA: Frontline Fellowship, 2009).
41. "Saudi Arabia," *The CIA World Factbook*, https://www.cia.gov/library/publications/the-world-factbook/geos/sa.html (accessed April 9, 2010).
42. Information available online at http://www.oic-oci.org/member_states.asp (accessed April 26, 2010).

### 5—A Vision of Islam
1. Information available online at http://www.jihadwatch.org/2006/11/germany-well-on-the-way-to-becoming-a-muslim-state-by-2050.html (accessed April 26, 2010).
2. Gaddafi quote available online at http://en.wikipedia.org/wiki/muammar_al-Gaddafi (accessed June 4, 2010).
3. Information available online at http://edition.cnn.com/video/#/video/world/2009/11/12/robertson.london.radicals.cnn (accessed April 26, 2010).
4. Omar Ahmad quote available online at http://en.wikipedia.org/wiki/Omar_Ahmad (accessed June 4, 2010).
5. Information available online at http://www.freedomhouse.org/uploads/special_report/45.pdf (accessed April 26, 2010).
6. Ibid.
7. Information available online at http://www.youtube.com/watch?v=15XcWLXMd7w; http://www.youtube.com/watch?v=f3WSb56Uq_w&NR=1; http://www.youtube.com/watch?v=YeTqheFnBM0&NR=1; http://www.youtube.com/watch#!v=qgL0HZ_-2pI&feature=related (accessed April 26, 2010).
8. Information available online at http://news.bbc.co.uk/2/hi/europe/7842344.stm (accessed April 26, 2010).
9. Information available online at http://www.youtube.com/watch?v=FckLO8HcNyo (accessed April 26, 2010).
10. Information available online at http://www.youtube.com/watch?v=92myDzAFgU4 (accessed April 26, 2010).
11. "Abortion Facts," The Center for Bio-Ethical Reform, http://www.abortionno.org/Resources/fastfacts.html (accessed April 12, 2010).

12. Ronald Kessler, "FBI: 10% of U.S. Mosques Preach Jihad," *Newsmax*, November 10, 2009, http://newsmax.com/RonaldKessler/Mosques-preach-jihad/2009/11/10/id/336125 (accessed April 12, 2010).

13. Ronald Reagan, quoted in Eugene C. Gerhart, ed., *Quote It Completely!* (Buffalo, NY: William S. Hein and Company, 1998), 958.

### 6—The Spirit of the Antichrist

1. Joel Richardson, *The Islamic Antichrist* (Washinton, DC: WND Books, 2009).

2. Abdulaziz, Abdulhussein, and Sachedina, *Islamic Messianism: The Idea of the Mahdi in Twelver Shi'ism* (Albany, NY: State University of New York Press, 1981).

3. Imam Muslim, *Al Jami-Us-Sahih* (n.p.: Muhammad Ashraf, 1992).

4. M.A. Veliankode, *Doomsday: Portents and Prophecies* (Scarborough, Ontario: Al-Attique Publishers, Inc. 1999), 351.

5. Imam Muslim, *Al Jami-Us-Sahih*.

6. Ayatullah Baqir al-Sadr and Ayatullah Murtada Mutahhar, *The Awaited Saviour* (Karachi, Pakistan: Islamic Seminary Publications, n.d.).

7. Mufti Mohammad Shafi, Muhammad Anwar Shah Kashmiri, Muhammad Rafi Usmani, and Rafiq Abdur Rehman, *Signs of Qiyamah and the Arrival of Maseeh* (n.p.: Darul Ishat, 2000), prologue.

8. S. Kamoonpuri, *Basic Beliefs of Islam* (n.p.: Tanzania Printers Limited, 2001), 42–58.

### 10—The Overcoming Church

1. Information available online at http://www.alligator.org/news/local/article_37395770-0a3c-11df-a650-001cc4c03286.html (accessed April 26, 2010).

2. Information available online at http://www.anglicansunited.com/?p=5729 (accessed April 26, 2010).

### 12—Stories Given for Our Learning

1. Information available online at http://news.bbc.co.uk/2/hi/uk_news/england/hampshire/7898972.stm (accessed April 26, 2010).

2. Information available online at http://info.kopp-verlag.de/news/deutschland-soll-malediven-bei-der-islamisierung-helfen.html (accessed April 26, 2010).

3. *Wikipedia*, s.v. "Martin Luther," http://en.wikipedia.org/wiki/Martin_Luther (accessed April 15, 2010).

4. Ibid.

### 13—The Church and the Government

1. Paul Steinhauser, "Poll: more disapprove of Bush than any other president," *CNNPolitics.com*, http://www.cnn.com/2008/POLITICS/05/01/bush.poll (accessed April 16, 2010).

2. Associated Press, "Worker: I was fired for wearing 'God' button," *MSNBC*, http://www.msnbc.msn.com/id/33505354 (accessed April 16, 2010).

3. Associated Press, "'Westernized' daughter case: Dad sent to Ariz.," *MSNBC*, http://www.msnbc.msn.com/id/33550176 (accessed April 16, 2010).

4. "Gunman Kills 12, Wounds 31 at Fort Hood," MSNBC, http://www.msnbc.msn.com/id/33678801/, accessed April 16, 2010. Wikipedia, s. v. "Fort Hood Shooting," http://en.wikipedia.org/wiki/Fort_Hood_shooting (accessed April 16, 2010).

5. Art Moore, "Should Muslim Quran Be USA's Top Authority?" *WorldNetDaily*, http://www.wnd.com/news/article.asp?ARTICLE_ID=32341 (accessed April 16, 2010).

6. Andrea Stone, "75 Percent of Young Americans Are Unfit for Military Duty," *AOL News*, http://www.aolnews.com/article/70-percent-of-young-americans-are-unfit-for-military-duty/19260560?icid=main (accessed April 16, 2010).

### 14—The Cost of Freedom

1. *Wikipedia*, s.v. "Pilgrim (Plymouth Colony)," http://en.wikipedia.org/wiki/Pilgrim_(Plymouth_Colony) (accessed April 16, 2010).

2. *Wikipedia*, s.v. "The Mayflower Society," http://en.wikipedia.org/wiki/Society_of_Mayflower_Descendants (accessed April 16, 2010).

3. *Wikipedia*, s.v. "Thanksgiving (United States)," http://en.wikipedia.org/wiki/Thanksgiving_(United_States) (accessed April 16, 2010).

4. *Wikipedia*, x.v. "Pledge of Allegiance," http://en.wikipedia.org/wiki/Pledge_of_Allegiance (accessed April 16, 2010).

### Appendix A—The Contrast Between Jesus Christ and Mohammed

1. *Sahih al-Bukhari*, Volume 8, Book 82, Number 806.

### Appendix B—Muslim Claims About the Quran

1. Ali Dashti, *Twenty-Three Years*.

2. James Hastings, *Encyclopedia of Religion and Ethics*.

3. Ibn Warraq, *Why I Am Not a Muslim*.

4. Ibn Warraq, *The Origins of the Koran: Classic Essays on Islam's Holy Book* (Amherst, NY: Prometheus Books, 1998).

5. Information available online at http://en.wikipedia.org/wiki/English_translations_of_the_Quran (accessed April 26, 2010).

### Appendix C—Blatant Errors in the Quran

1. Ibn Warraq, *The Origins of the Koran: Classic Essays on Islam's Holy Book* (Amherst, NY: Prometheus Books, 1998).

### To Contact the Author
info@doveworld.org